Death Rehearsal

© Doug Pokorski 1995

First published in the United States of America in 1995 by:

    Octavo Press (an imprint of Templegate Publishers)
    302 East Adams Street
    P.O. Box 5152
    Springfield, Illinois
    62705-5152

ISBN 0-87243-215-7

Library of Congress Catalog Card Number 95-60159

Cover: Edward Hopper's *Rooms by the Sea*
Yale University Art Gallery
Bequest of Stephen Carlton Clark, B.A. 1903

Death Rehearsal:
A Practical Guide for Preparing for the Inevitable

by
Doug Pokorski

Octavo Press
An imprint of Templegate Publishers
Springfield, Illinois

This book is dedicated with love to my parents
Robert J. Pokorski (1920 – 1991)
and
Jeanne V. Pokorski

Contents

Introduction

This is a book about what to do when someone has died. It is not a book about coping with grief. That is an intensely personal problem, one which each person will find his or her answer to. This book is about dealing with death as a job of work, about those things that must be done in the event that someone close to you dies — an event that is bound to happen to virtually all of us, probably more than once.

Some people might find it a bit cold to contemplate the details of dealing with death the way you might think about framing a picture or getting a new roof put on your house. Others might find some temporary solace in focusing on the nuts and bolts details of dealing with death rather than dwelling on the feelings surrounding a deep personal loss. Either way, when someone close has died, there are things that must be done, and it will be best if they are done efficiently and well.

I suspect that as recently as a generation or two ago a book like this not only would have been unnecessary, but might even have seemed rather ludicrous. For most of our history, we Americans mostly lived in communities where we knew and were known by the people around us — communities where the social system for dealing with death could be counted on to kick in automatically and quite effectively whenever needed. Questions such as those addressed in this book were quickly addressed by friends, family, fellow members of religious congregations and professionals, all of whom were familiar with the needs of the bereaved and well-versed in what needed to be done and how it could be best accomplished.

Even today, many of us still live in such communities. In my own family, for example, my ancestors have been buried by the same two or three funeral homes in Lincoln, Illinois, for the better part of a century. The remains of family members who died in the 1880s lie only gravestones apart from those who died in the 1990s.

When my father died a few years ago, the arrangements were handled by the same funeral home that buried his mother in 1978, his father in 1957 and his grandmother in 1942. The funeral was held in the church where he had been baptized 70 years earlier, served as an altar boy, been married and attended services nearly every Sunday since the end of World War II. It was the same church — not just the same congregation, but the same red brick building — from which his parents and grandparents had been buried over the course of nearly a century.

For the most part, in dealing with the details of his death, my family never had to ask "What do we do now?" There were familiar figures on hand — priests, funeral directors, friends — who knew what had to come next and could ease our way through the process.

That's why, when it was first suggested that I write this book, I had to stop and ask myself who would be interested in reading it. "Don't most people already know all that stuff?" I wondered. It took me a while to realize that a large number of Americans, quite possibly a sizeable majority, are not so fortunate as to have a well developed network in place to help when a loved one dies and have little, if any, personal knowledge of dealing with death to fall back on.

Because of our society's incredible mobility, they may live in communities where they are largely strangers, where even the location of the local funeral homes and cemeteries may be unknown to them, where their local priest, minister or rabbi is a virtual stranger and where the town's funeral directors are ominous figures whose motives are highly suspect. For them, the question of what needs to be done in the event of a death may present an array of problems they have never previously addressed.

It is for people in that situation that I hope this book will be most beneficial. It is meant to be a practical guide, and, for that reason, there are some aspects of dealing with death that you won't find here. You will not, for example, find any discussion of cryogenics. If you have a serious interest in the idea of having your head frozen in liquid nitrogen after you die so that it can be reanimated 200 years hence and fastened atop a newly manufactured body of surpassing physical perfection, this is not the place to pursue it. Nor will you find any information on recently reported efforts by some people to recreate ancient Egyptian mummification techniques. If your vanity is such that it is important to you that your body be preserved for thousands of years, you will have to look elsewhere for guidance.

You will, I hope, find in this book useful, practical information concerning the kinds of things you will have to deal with when a loved one dies and some practical suggestions as to how best to cope with them. In writing it, I found myself drawing fairly extensively on my own background in dealing with death. As a child, I was blessed to live in an area which included an abundance of relatives, many of them elderly. I probably attended my first wake and funeral about the time I started school, and I know I helped pick out my grandfather's casket when he died when I was about six.

If my experiences from an early age with the details of dealing with death have been valuable, they have also tended to impose a limited perspective on my understanding of the topic — that of traditional Christian burial customs in a reasonably traditional small town in the midwest. I have tried to broaden that point of view and the base of knowledge that goes with it by researching a wide array of sources. In the process, I have discovered a great deal that I didn't know, ranging from how to be an informed consumer in dealing with the funeral industry, to what to be sure to ask about when having a body cremated, to things the living can do to make their own deaths easier on their survivors, to the vital importance of being willing to be an organ and tissue donor.

In the process of researching and writing the book I've also answered my original question "Who would be interested in reading it?" or at least "Who can benefit from reading it?" I think the answer is "An awful lot of people." I hope you're one of them.

Acknowledgements and special thanks

A number of individuals and organizations have been most helpful in the preparation of this manuscript, and their assistance is deeply and sincerely appreciated. I never fail to be impressed by the willingness of so many people to give generously of their time and energy when called by a stranger half a continent away who says "I'm working on a book and I need some information. Can you help me?"

At the same time, it is important to emphasize here that none of those sources is responsible for any errors of fact in this book or any inaccuracies it may inadvertently contain, and certainly not for the point of view it expresses. That responsibility belongs to the author alone.

That being said, I would like to give special thanks first to my wife, Diana Lehmann, for her help in getting this book together. Without her assistance in researching this manuscript, I doubt that I would have been able to finish it, and I know I would not have been able to finish it within any reasonable time frame. Her assistance in reading and helping to edit the text as it was being written was also invaluable, and her unflagging support and encouragement and her considerable patience helped make this a very enjoyable project for me.

Others who have been most helpful in researching this book include Jeff Lair, coroner of Morgan County, Ill., and secretary of the Illinois Coroners and Medical Examiners Association; Robert W. Ninker, executive director of the Illinois Funeral Directors Association; Andrea Suddeth, curator of the American Funeral Service Museum; Elizabeth Hager, coordinator for the organ donor program for Illinois Secretary of State George Ryan; Bill Peithmann, an attorney and expert in estate planning in Farmer City, Ill.; Marian Blake, of the Continental Association of Funeral and Memorial Societies, Inc.; Sue Daniels, of the National Funeral Directors Association; Nyda Budig, press officer at the Bureau of Consular Affairs in the U.S. State Department; Rabbi Yosef Lefowitz, Piser Temple, Weinstein Memorial Chapel, Chicago, Ill.; Rabbi Barry Marks, Temple Israel, Springfield, Ill.; Lorraine Willmott, Communications Specialist, Regional Organ Bank of Illinois (ROBI); Larry Aut, Director of Research Services, Southern Illinois University School of Medicine; Jack M. Springer, Executive Director of The Cremation Society of North America.

Thanks for information are due to the American Association of Retired Persons; the Funeral Service Consumer Assistance Program of the National Research and Information Center; the Illinois State Bar Association; Federated Funeral Directors of America; Camp Butler National Cemetery and the U.S. Department of Veterans Affairs; Oak Ridge Cemetery, Springfield, Ill.; the Cremation Society of Illinois; and the Anatomical Gift Association of Illinois.

Chapter I
The first few hours

We humans have been coping with the deaths of those near and dear to us at least since the days when one Neanderthal would turn to another Neanderthal and say something like "You know, Uncle Ogg hasn't moved at all in several days. I don't think he'll be making the big hunt with us next week. And we should probably do something about getting him out of the cave."

Certainly, a death can be the occasion of feelings of great sadness and loss, a sense of our own mortality and even sometimes feelings of guilt. Just as importantly, however, death is also a time when things must be done. Decisions must be made, actions must be taken.

Yet, every few years we read or hear on the news about some poor soul whose aged parent, say, has passed away and who has left the body just as it was in the front bedroom, perhaps even talking to it and tending the body as if it were still alive. But such sad cases only serve to underline the fact that when we are faced with the death of someone close to us, procrastination and indecision are not really options. What follows is a guide for what decisions need to be made, what actions need to be taken and what options really do exist for the survivors.

First, Make Sure

In just the first few hours after the death of someone close to you, it is critical that certain things be done. The first is to make sure that what you are dealing with is in fact a death.

This probably won't be a problem if the person has died in a hospital, nursing home or other institution where trained medical personnel will be on hand to confirm the sad fact. Nor is it likely to be an issue in the case of a person who has been in a hospice with a terminal disease. Even if death takes place at home, if the person has been ill or is of advanced age and in frail health, there is likely to be little doubt that they are indeed dead.

In some cases, though, death may come as a complete surprise. While professional funeral directors will tell you that "dead is dead and you know it when you see it," it may not always be so easy to tell, even for trained professionals. An extreme example of both lay people and experienced professionals being mistaken about a condition that appeared to be death but was not occurred in Albany, N.Y., in November of 1994. An 86-year-old woman was found motionless in her nightgown on the floor of her apartment living room. The woman's skin was blue and, to the apartment manager who found her, she appeared dead. Police and fire department rescue personnel who were called to the scene also believed the woman to be dead. The county coroner was called and he found no signs of life — no breathing, pulse or heartbeat. The coroner, who was not a doctor, later told the media that the woman's body was stiff and as cold as ice. The woman was taken to the local morgue and put in a cooler in which the temperature was forty degrees fahrenheit. After about ninety minutes in the cooler, a morgue supervisor removed the body to have it ready for the funeral director, who was coming to pick it up. Much to his astonishment, the supervisor then noticed that the woman was breathing. The woman was not dead at all. She was revived and made, according to news reports, a brief, if incomplete recovery. She died a second and final time about a week later.

There have also been a number of reports over the years of drowning victims, particularly victims who drowned in very cold water, being revived and making good recoveries after appearing to be dead. While such cases are rare, they are reason enough to call emergency personnel first when, for example, you come home to find a spouse or family member unexpectedly collapsed and apparently dead on the floor.

In many parts of the country, all it takes to summon emergency help is to call 911. Elsewhere, call the police, emergency medical squad, fire department, or your family physician. These numbers should be posted on or next to your phone. As a last resort, simply dial the operator. Depending on who you call and who responds, you could wind up being billed, of course, but it will be a small price to pay for the peace of mind of knowing that you did not overlook even the small possibility that someone who appeared to be dead was actually alive.

A Vital Gift

Once you are sure that what you're dealing with really is death, certain decisions must be made fairly quickly. If you are not the next of kin of the deceased, or you do not have legal authorization to act in place of the next of kin, the first step should be to notify the appropriate relative.

If you are the next of kin or have legal authorization to act in that capacity, you must make two relatively quick decisions about the immediate disposition of the body. Potentially the most important is whether any of the deceased's organs or tissues will be donated for transplants or medical research.

One of the greatest gifts many of us ever will be able to offer to anyone else is the donation of a heart, kidney, cornea or other body part for transplantation. In the case of some organs, such as hearts and livers, a transplant can literally make the difference between life and death. In 1994 it was estimated that more than 2,800 people were waiting for heart transplants alone, and that a third of them, more than 950 people, would die for lack of donated hearts.

In other cases, donated organs and tissues can make the difference between leading a normal life or being severely restricted, for example, by blindness, being tied to a kidney dialysis machine or by being unable to walk. Donated organs and tissues replace malfunctioning kidneys and corneas, help speed healing in burn victims, promote bone regrowth in people suffering from serious bone disease and mend damaged knees and other joints in athletes and others who have been injured.

Organs and tissues that commonly are transplanted include the kidney, heart, liver, pancreas, lung, small bowel, bone, bone marrow, heart valves, some veins, corneas, cartilage, ligaments and skin. Organ and tissue recovery can be done at almost all of the nation's hospitals.

Organs, including the heart, liver and kidney, can only be donated from someone who has been declared "brain dead." That is, although the person is truly dead, the organs to be transplanted are still alive. All brain function has irreversibly ceased, but the heart, lungs, circulatory system and so on are kept functioning in a hospital by the use of mechanical devices. For that reason, most organ donors are people who have died as the result of some trauma such as a car accident or other violent incident after which they were taken to a hospital quickly and their vital functions were sustained artificially.

Artificial maintenance of body functions is not necessary in donated tissues, such as corneas, bones and skin. Tissue can be donated in cases where the heart and lungs of the deceased have completely stopped functioning and cannot be revived. It is worth noting that in such cases, while organs like the heart cannot be donated because they have suffered irreversible damage, tissue such as heart valves can still be salvaged.

Some organs for transplantation, such as the heart, are normally taken only from younger donors to ensure that the organs are in the best condition possible. Because organs for transplant must be matched for size and other factors, even very young children can be donors. There are no upper age limits for the donation of some tissues, such as corneas. Organs and tissue that cannot be used for transplants may be used for medical research.

There are few limits on who can be a donor, although organs and tissue are not recovered in the case of homicide. People who die of cancer or infectious diseases, including AIDS, cannot be donors.

Depending on which organs and tissues may be involved, time is a crucial factor if a person is to be a donor. In most cases, organs or tissues must be removed within 24 to 36 hours of the time of death. As a result, the decision whether or not to make a persons organs and tissue available for transplant should be made as soon as possible after death, if not beforehand. Under federal law, personnel at almost every hospital in the country must ask the families of potential organ and tissue donors to consider donating.

Many people will have already made up their own minds about whether they want to be organ and tissue donors. Many states provide a Uniform Donor Card on the reverse side of drivers licenses. If the driver signs the card, along with two witnesses to the signature, it is an indication of that person's wish to be a donor. Other people may carry a separate Uniform Donor Card. Either form of the card includes three options for donation — the donation of any and all organs and tissues that are useable, the donation of specific organs and/or tissues and the donation of the body for medical research. However, if organs or tissue are removed for transplantation, the body cannot then be donated for medical research.

A sample Uniform Donor Card that can be photocopied and carried in your wallet or purse is printed in this book on page 149, along with additional information about donated organs, tissue, and bodies.

The presence of a signed Uniform Donor Card is a clear indication of the wishes of the deceased, but it is by no means a guarantee that those wishes will be carried out. The consent of the next of kin also is required before organs or tissues can be donated. Of course, in the absence of an organ donor card or any other sign of the wishes of the deceased, the next of kin also can decide to donate the organs and tissues.

Although the survivors of someone who dies will be expected to pay medical costs for the person's care when he or she was alive, there is no additional cost to the survivors connected with donating organs and tissue. There have been instances when hospitals have erroneously billed the family of the deceased for removing organs and tissues, but those errors have usually been promptly rectified. Insurance companies, Medicare or the recipients themselves pay for the cost of removing organs and of transplantation. Just as doctors and hospitals cannot legally charge the families of donors for any costs related to transplantation, it is also illegal for the families of donors to receive any payment for the donation.

Agreeing to be an organ donor, or to have the organs of a relative donated, does not effect the quality of medical care the person receives. By law, doctors involved in transplanting organs cannot be the same doctors who care for the patient donating the organs, nor are they allowed to influence the decision to cut off artificial life support.

Once the needed organs and tissues have been removed, the remains are released to the family for the funeral and burial. The body is not disfigured by the removal of most organs and tissues. In cases where there are visible signs of the surgery to remove organs and tissues, the doctors performing the surgery will take reconstructive measures to eliminate any disfiguration. That means that an open casket funeral is always possible where organs and tissues have been donated, unless there was other major damage to the body prior to the transplant surgery.

According to the American Council on Transplantation, most religions, including Catholicism, Judaism and the various Protestant denominations, support organ and tissue donation. Most others treat it as a personal decision, while a few have reservations about specific aspects of the process. Islam, for example, permits organ transplantation provided the donor consents in writing before death and that the organs be transplanted immediately and not stored in organ banks. One of the few ethnic/religious groups that opposes donation are Gypsies, who believe that the body of a dead person must remain intact because the person's soul maintains the physical shape of the body as the soul retraces the steps of the deceased for one year after death.

If the deceased has signed a Uniform Donor Card or otherwise indicated clearly a desire to donate organs and tissues, it would seem best for the next of kin to honor those wishes by consenting to the donation. Similarly, if the deceased had clearly expressed an opposition to the idea of organ or tissue donation, those wishes should also be respected. Where the feelings of the deceased are unclear or unknown, the next of kin will have to let their own consciences guide them.

Polls have shown that most Americans think it's a good idea that donated organs and tissue are available in case such transplant material is needed for themselves or their family members. A much smaller number, however, have signed Uniform Donor Cards and agreed to be donors themselves. The potential benefits to others from organ and tissue donation is tremendous. Transplanted kidneys, hearts and other organs can add twenty to thirty years to the lives of people suffering from serious diseases. Skin, bone, corneas and other tissue from a single donor can help many, many people in need. With the need for donations of body parts for transplants exceeding the supply by as much as two to one in some cases, and in the absence of strong religious or other personal convictions to the contrary, it's hard to justify *not* agreeing to be a donor or to donate material from a deceased loved one.

Separate arrangements are sometimes made to donate a body for use as a cadaver in teaching or research to a specific medical school or organization representing a group of medical schools. This kind of arrangement is best made in advance in consultation with the school or association. It can be difficult, or even prohibitively impractical, for the next of kin to try to make such arrangements at the time of death, although it is possible. As an example of the kinds of difficulties you might encounter, even when arrangements have been made in advance, a given medical school may not have a need for bodies for teaching or research at the time of death, and may refuse to accept the deceased.

Where a person has made arrangements prior to death, it is important to contact the medical school or association quickly to find out if the body will be accepted and what procedures should be followed to convey it to the appropriate location. The responsibility for the cost of transportation in such cases may be the family's or it may be borne by the medical school or association.

Bodies donated for medical research should not be embalmed using the conventional techniques employed by most funeral homes. A body donated for research may be kept for a few months up to more than a year, and conventional embalming will not be effective that long. Medical schools use special methods of long term preservation.

When a medical school or other institution is finished with a body, the remains usually are cremated. If previous arrangements have been made with the institution, the ashes can be returned to the family, usually by mail.

Removal of the body.

Once a decision has been reached concerning the donation of organs, tissues or the entire body, some other immediate decisions remain. Of course, if the entire body has been donated, you won't have to worry about further decisions on the disposition of the remains, at least not for some time. A more likely situation, however, is that the body, with or without transplantable organs and tissue, remains to be dealt with. If you have decided against organ and tissue donation, you will have to decide on your next step rather quickly, and even if time is allowed to recover organs and tissues for transplantation, that only delays the decision by a few hours.

If the body is at home, you will probably want to have it removed fairly soon, although some people find that it helps the grieving process if it remains in the home for a while. If the person died at a nursing home, it will be in the best interests of the other patients to have the body removed quickly. Most hospitals will have facilities to store the body for a time, and a refrigerated body can be kept almost indefinitely, but they probably will prefer that it is removed as soon as possible. The hospital may also charge an additional fee for storage of the body.

Almost invariably, at some point in the first few hours, you will need to contact someone to remove the body, and that someone almost certainly will be a funeral director. Dealing with funeral directors will be discussed more fully in the next chapter. For the time being, however, a few facts are important. For most deaths, the services of a funeral director will be needed, although there is ample room for debate as to how extensive those services should be. It is possible in many states to handle virtually all aspects of dealing with a death yourself, but that kind of ultimate do-it-yourself project is probably only of interest to a very few people.

If your family has used the services of a local funeral director before, and if the service has been satisfactory, you will probably use that person or firm again. Although it may seem a little odd, since each of us (with the possible exception of Shirley Maclaine) experiences death only once, about eighty percent of the business funeral directors do in this country is repeat business. Families return to the same funeral home, again and again as the need presents itself unless they have found its services wanting in the past.

If you don't have a funeral director you are familiar with, perhaps because you have moved away from the community where your family lives, it is best to ask friends, co-workers, business associates or other acquaintances for recommendations. If the deceased was an actively religious person, that may help make the decision easier. Even small communities typically have funeral homes that tend to "specialize" based on the religious preference of their clientele. In most communities, for example, just about anyone can tell you which is the Catholic funeral home, and which one is the Protestant one, and there may even be distinctions among Protestant denominations. If you are in a smaller town, you may need to look to a nearby larger city for a funeral director who deals mainly with clients of the Jewish or Muslim faith.

In rare cases, some affiliation other than religion may influence the choice of a funeral director. For example, when a former Republican congressman and cabinet member died in 1994, he was buried from his hometown Catholic church, but the arrangements were handled by a funeral director who more often handles the funerals of Protestants. The town's Catholic funeral director was an active Democrat, while the owner of the "Protestant" funeral home was a Republican office holder.

Once you have the name of three or four possible funeral directors, go to the phone and call them. Ask about their prices, or the price ranges for typical services. Under federal law, such information must be available over the telephone. Don't worry too much about making comparisons down to the last dollar and cent. You will have a chance to sit down and look at a detailed list of prices later. At this point you want to get a general feel for cost as well as a sense of what kind of people you are dealing with. If the staff at the other end of the line is quick to answer your questions in full, that's a good sign as opposed to someone who seems uninformed or unwilling to be aboveboard about prices for merchandise and service.

Also ask about the location of the funeral home. If all other factors are equal, it may be an advantage to pick a funeral home that is located near the cemetery where burial will take place and/or the church or other facility where services will be held.

If you are faced with a situation where you must choose a funeral director quickly to remove and take charge of a body, and if you are completely at a loss as to whom to choose, don't panic. Even if you make a choice more or less at random right after the time of death, you probably won't have any major problems. All you have to do is authorize the funeral director to remove the body to his or her place of business and to do nothing further except hold the body until you have had a chance to come into the funeral home and discuss procedures and prices.

When you do go to the funeral home, probably within the next twenty-four hours or so, you will have time to evaluate the funeral director and his place of business and perhaps ask friends and acquaintances what they have heard about the establishment's reputation. If you decide that you don't like what you see or hear about the funeral director, you are well within your rights to shop around, find a funeral home you like better, and request that establishment to take over the remainder of the arrangements.

Of course, you will owe the first funeral director for whatever services were actually performed, but you are in no way obligated to allow that person to continue with the rest of the arrangements.

If the deceased was a member of a funeral or memorial society, that, too, will simplify the choice of funeral director. Such organizations, which are discussed in greater detail in chapter VII, usually employ the services of a limited number of funeral directors. Again, if you don't know if the deceased was a member of a funeral or memorial society and you must arrange to move the body, you can always call one funeral director for your immediate need, then switch to another affiliated with a memorial society later.

Whom to Notify First

Another important task in the first few hours after a death is to notify those people closest to the deceased, as well as those closest to the survivors. While there are no hard and fast rules here, a certain amount of common sense does apply. Except for extreme cases where family members are estranged, the immediate family should be notified right away, no matter what the time. People generally feel better when they are told of a death as soon as possible, even in the middle of the night, rather than having to wait until hours later. Parents, brothers and sisters, spouses should be contacted quickly. The same is true for very close friends. An exception might be made in the case of someone who is seriously ill or for some other reason might suffer a major negative reaction to being told of the death. In such cases, it may be best to consult with other friends or family members to decide on the best way to break the news.

In general, however, it's probably best to notify someone of a death in the simplest and most straightforward way possible. When death is sudden and unexpected, there is no easy way to tell someone what has happened. No effort to cushion the blow can really be effective, and a clumsy attempt to provide a calming or reassuring lead in the announcement itself can actually increase the anxiety felt by the person you are talking to. In cases where death is not unexpected, where old age or a longterm disease is the cause, for example, the shock of being told about it may not be as great, but the straightforward approach is still probably the best. In either case, when telling someone of death, you should get to the point quickly and say simply what has happened. If you are notifying someone by telephone that a relative has died, for example, something along the following lines would be a good approach.

"Hello, Susan, this is your cousin, Doug. I hope I'm not disturbing you, but I'm afraid I have some bad news. Uncle Bob died last night."

In making your notifications, be sure to give prompt notice to friends and relatives who live at some distance from where the funeral or other service will be held. Those people who may wish to come to the service will probably need as much advance notice as they can get to make the necessary arrangements.

As the person making the arrangements and dealing most directly with the death, it is important for your own well-being to notify your own inner circle of friends as soon as possible. Brothers or sisters, close supportive friends or others who will want to offer their assistance will be grateful if they are contacted quickly, and you will be equally grateful for the support they give.

Don't worry about notifying everybody who needs to be told right away. Once a few people have been called, they will begin to pass on the word, and you can make arrangements to be sure everyone who needs to know is contacted later.

However, another key person to call, if the deceased was, or the survivors are, at all religious, is the appropriate member of the clergy. If the deceased had a priest, minister, rabbi or other religious leader that he or she routinely turned to for spiritual comfort and guidance, call that person right away. Or as an alternative, call the member of the clergy who fills that role in your own life. Prompt notification of a member of the clergy may be especially important if the deceased was Jewish. Traditional Jewish custom generally requires that burial take place shortly after death, usually before the next sunset, so arrangements must be made quickly.

Again, don't hesitate to call a member of the clergy because of the lateness of the hour. Providing comfort at a time of death is an expected duty for the clergy, and most priests, ministers and rabbis will gladly come at any time to aid a member of their congregation.

Also, be sure that someone is called on to take care of any minor children or other dependents, such as an elderly relative who might have been living with the deceased. Such individuals will need someone to look out for their immediate physical needs as well as to comfort them at their time of loss.

Pets may also need to be looked after immediately. Dogs and cats, in particular, don't do well if they are left for long without care, while other pets, such as birds and fish, will need to be fed and tended to. Even if there are no children or pets involved, someone also should be deputized to keep an eye on the house or apartment of the deceased. In addition to the concern of security there may be houseplants that need to be tended, heating, air conditioning or plumbing to be adjusted and telephone messages to be checked.

Checklist

☐ If death is unexpected, call family doctor, 911 or other emergency numbers.

☐ Determine if deceased signed a Uniform Donor card. If not, next of kin must decide whether to approve donation.

☐ Contact funeral director to arrange for removal of body.

☐ Notify next of kin, other close friends and relatives. Also notify geographically distant friends and relatives who may need to make travel plans to attend the services.

☐ Arrange for someone to take charge of minor children, if necesary.

☐ Arrange for someone to check the home of the deceased, take care of pets, house plants, utilities, etc.

Chapter II
What to do the first day or two

First of all, don't take the title of this chapter *too* literally. Yes, in most situations the decisions and actions to be discussed here will be dealt with in the first day or so after a person has died. However, there are exceptions to the rules in any line of human endeavor, and that can certainly be true of dealing with death. For example, if there is a large and geographically far-flung family in which several members want to take an active role in arranging the services, burial and other matters, it may be necessary to postpone taking some of the first steps for several days or longer. That should not present a major problem in most cases. A body can be kept refrigerated indefinitely, providing the funeral director has refrigeration facilities. Even in the absence of refrigeration facilities, dry ice may be used to keep the body cold. If refrigeration is not an option for the funeral director you are dealing with, it may be necessary to find one who does have refrigeration capability or to decide on embalming right away. If you go ahead with embalming, you can still wait a few days before making other decisions.

Ordinarily, however, there are a number of steps that you will need to take within the first day or two after a death has occurred.

Meeting With the Funeral Director

In most cases, you will have already selected a funeral director and made an initial contact, but you probably will not have made all the decisions you will need to make or gone into all the details you will need to consider until you pay a visit to the funeral home to discuss your plans. This is your opportunity to get answers to any questions you have and, if you have any doubts at all remaining, to satisfy yourself that you wish to continue with this particular funeral director.

At this point it is probably a good idea to point out that a lot that has been written and broadcast about the funeral industry in the last thirty years or so has tended to villainize funeral directors as a group. Beginning at least in 1963 with Jessica Mitford's exposé "The American Way of Death," funeral directors have frequently been portrayed as predators bent on foisting unneeded, unwanted and overpriced services on unwary people who are under great emotional stress and are at their most vulnerable. Certainly ample evidence has been presented that at least some funeral directors and others in the industry have behaved that badly, or worse. It is also true that funeral directors, like doctors, dentists, lawyers, plumbers, grocers, auto mechanics, and many others are in business to make money and employ strategies designed to enhance their profits.

That being said, there does not seem any reason to believe that funeral directors as a group are any more reprehensible or less honorable and decent than any of those other groups of professionals. They do provide a valuable and needed service. Critics who argue that American funeral customs are almost totally the result of the manipulation of a profit-driven funeral industry seem to overlook the cultural and human roots that underlie the modern desire to honor, commemorate and celebrate the dead.

In that perspective, meeting with a funeral director should not be viewed as an encounter with someone out to take advantage of you, nor should it be seen as an occasion to put yourself blindly into the hands of someone whose motives are totally altruistic. Rather, as an informed consumer, approach the situation with as much knowledge as you can muster and with the attitude that you are no more likely to be taken advantage of than the funeral director would be likely to be taken advantage of by you. Know, too, that if you do not want to incorporate any or all the elements of a "typical" or "traditional' funeral in your own plans, you are free to make that decision, even to the extent of burying the deceased in your back yard yourself. (More about that in Chapter VI.)

One important tool you have as an informed consumer is a set of guidelines governing pricing and other disclosures set by the Federal Trade Commission in the FTC Funeral Rule, which went into effect in 1984 and was and updated in July of 1994. Prompted in part by earlier criticisms of the funeral industry, the Funeral Rule requires funeral directors in the United States to give consumers accurate itemized prices and other information about funeral goods and services. It also prohibits misrepresentation of legal, crematory and cemetery requirements; embalming for a fee without permission; requiring the purchase of a casket for a direct cremation; requiring the purchase of certain funeral goods or services as a condition for furnishing other goods or services and engaging in other deceptive practices. Funeral directors who violate the Funeral Rule may be subject to penalties of up to $10,000 per violation. The rule applies not only to licensed funeral directors but to cemeteries, crematories and other businesses that prepare and care for bodies; arrange, supervise or conduct ceremonies associated with death and sell goods to the public in connection with death services. The rule applies to funeral planning made at the time of death as well as to so called "pre-need" planning, in which healthy, relatively young persons make arrangements for their own funerals at some indeterminate point in the future.

Under the Funeral Rule, a funeral director must give you a General Price List as soon as you and he have your first face to face meeting in which you begin to discuss the type of funeral or other disposition of the remains, the specific goods and services that he offers or the prices of his goods and services. Such a face to face conversation does not have to take place in a funeral home for the rule to apply. It could take place at a hospital or nursing home, for example, and the terms of the Funeral Rule must still be observed.

An exception is allowed if a funeral director is simply removing the deceased from the place of death to a funeral home and asking for permission to embalm the body. He does not have to give you a full price list at that time, but he is required to inform you that embalming is not required by law, except in some very limited circumstances, and he is not allowed to discuss prices any further at that time unless he provides a General Price List, or GPL.

The rule requires that certain items must be included on the GPL, and that you must be offered your own copy of the list, free of charge. In fact, anyone who comes to a funeral director in person and asks must be given a copy of the list free of charge. The rule also requires that a funeral director give accurate information from his GPL and other pricing information over the telephone to anyone who asks whether they identify themselves or not.

The GPL must include the name, address, and telephone number of the business and the effective date of the price list. It must inform consumers that they have the right to select only the items they wish to purchase, apart from a basic services fee, which covers items such as securing death certificates and other documents, holding the body until disposition, meeting with the family, and overhead costs. The consumer cannot decline the basic services fee.

You must be informed, through the GPL, that embalming is not required by law except in special circumstances, such as in the case of death by certain contagious diseases or where the body must be transported to another state or country. However, embalming may legally be required for certain funeral arrangements, as when the casket will be open for a formal viewing of the body. You must also be informed that other funeral arrangements — direct cremation or immediate burial — are possible without having the body embalmed. You must be told that if you choose cremation, a formal casket or coffin is not needed and that you may choose an alternative, and less expensive container, to hold the body for and during cremation.

The GPL must also include the items covered by the non-declinable basic services fee, and must inform you that itemized listings of prices for caskets and cemetery burial containers are available for inspection at the funeral home. It must also indicate that vaults or other burial containers are not required by law in most states or localities, but that many cemeteries require some type of burial vault or grave liner to prevent grave subsidence.

Itemized prices must be provided for sixteen specific goods and services:

1. Forwarding remains to another funeral home.

2. Receiving remains from another funeral home.

3. Direct Cremation. This includes the funeral home's charge for the services involved with cremation. If a separate crematory will be used, the GPL should indicate that there will be an additional charge for the actual cremation.

4. Immediate burial. Again, this includes the funeral director's charges but does not cover cemetery costs.

5. Basic services and overhead. If you choose either a direct cremation or a direct burial, a basic services and overhead charge must be included in the pricing for those items, and the funeral director is not allowed to add a separate and additional basic services and overhead charge to the bill.

6. Transfer of remains from the place of death to the funeral home.

7. Embalming. In embalming, the mouth, nose and other openings are closed, then body fluids are drained through a vein while embalming fluids, which slow decomposition, are injected into the body through one or more arteries.

8. Other preparation of the body, including cosmetic work to prepare the body for viewing in an open casket ceremony. This may also include a price for washing and disinfecting the body, when that procedure is used instead of embalming.

9. Use of the funeral director's facilities and staff for a viewing of the remains.

10. Use of facilities and staff for a funeral service. A separate price should be listed for the services of staff at a location other than the funeral home, such as a church.

11. Use of facilities and staff for a memorial service. The difference between a funeral service and a memorial service is that in a funeral, the remains are present, while a memorial service takes place without the body being present, usually after burial or cremation.

12. Use of facilities and staff for a graveside service. The separate price listing for a graveside service is intended for those situations when there is no funeral at the funeral home or elsewhere. The listing for the price for a funeral ceremony should indicate whether a graveside service is included or list a separate fee for such a service.

13. The cost for the use of a hearse to transport the body.

14. The cost for the use of one or more limousines to transport mourners.

15. Either a listing of individual casket prices or a range of prices that are listed on the separate casket price list.

16. Either a listing of individual outer burial container prices or a range of prices that appear on a separate outer burial container price list.

It is not legal for a funeral director to list any of these sixteen items as being "free." The cost of items listed as "free" is invariably recovered elsewhere in a bill, so the FTC requires funeral directors to specify actual charges where they occur, rather than concealing them. Samples of price lists appear in the appendix on pages 141 – 146.

In addition to the General Price List, the funeral director may provide alternative price lists for special groups, such as religious groups and memorial societies that have entered into agreements to set special prices for their members. A separate price list may also be provided in the case of the deaths of infants and children.

The FTC Funeral Rule also specifically prohibits misrepresentation by funeral directors or their employees in six specific areas: embalming, cremation, outer burial containers, legal and cemetery requirements, claims about the preservation or protection of the body, and cash advance items.

As we have said, it is a violation of the rule for a funeral director to tell you that embalming is required by state or local law when that is not true. Any special local laws or regulations regarding embalming also must be spelled out in the GPL. (There is no federal law which requires embalming.) When embalming is not required by law, it is a violation of the Funeral Rule to say that embalming is required for "practical purposes" when you want a direct cremation or an immediate burial, or when refrigeration is available and a closed casket funeral with no formal viewing or visitation is desired.

In the case of an immediate burial with no formal viewing, a funeral director may not legally claim that embalming is required if you or other mourners want to lift the lid of the casket for a final, brief look at the deceased. A brief final look does not constitute a formal viewing and does not require embalming. When the family declines embalming, they cannot be required to pay for cosmetic work or other items considered on the GPL as "other preparation of the body."

Nor can a funeral director claim that state or local law requires a casket for a direct cremation — that is, a cremation which occurs without any formal viewing of the remains or any visitation or ceremony with the body present. It is also a violation of the rule to tell consumers that they are required to buy a casket for any other reason in the case of direct cremation. Most crematories do require some kind of container to facilitate the handling of the remains, but such "alternative containers" are far less expensive than caskets. They are usually made of materials such as unfinished wood, fiberboard or composition materials, without ornamentation or a fixed lining. They may come with an outside covering, or they may be without a covering. Crematories are also prohibited from requiring the purchase of a casket for a direct cremation, but they are allowed to set standards for the kinds of alternative containers they will accept.

A funeral director cannot legally claim that a burial vault or other outer burial container is required by state or local law if that is not true. In fact, the funeral director must specifically inform you when the law does not require outer burial containers. You must also be told that simple concrete slab grave liners are as acceptable as the more expensive outer burial vaults in meeting any requirements for outer burial containers established by law or the regulations of an individual cemetery. Funeral providers also are prohibited by the Funeral Rule from claiming that any law or any cemetery requires the purchase of an item or service when that is not true.

Funeral providers cannot legally claim that embalming or any other funeral goods or services will delay the natural decomposition of the body for a long or indefinite period of time. The main purpose of modern embalming is to prevent noticeable decomposition for the few days that normally transpire between death and funeral services. The more elaborate method of embalming used by medical schools to prepare cadavers for use in research can preserve bodies for up to a year. It must be said, however that now-abandoned techniques and chemicals that were once used for embalming had fairly amazing abilities to preserve the dead. For example, after President Abraham Lincoln was assassinated in 1865, his body had to be prepared to endure a series of public ceremonies and a long train trip with many stops from Washington D.C. to Springfield, Illinois. Powerful chemicals were used which essentially mummified or petrified Lincoln's corpse. The results were so successful that when his body was examined in 1901, following the rebuilding of his tomb in Springfield's Oak Ridge Cemetery, observers reported that it was remarkably intact and well-preserved.

In more modern times, there have been some examples of equally effective embalming. For example, when assassinated

41

civil rights leader Medgar Evers' body was exhumed in the 1990s, some 30 years after his death, he reportedly looked as if he had been buried only recently. However, most modern embalming is not designed to perform such miracles. Its purpose is to allow formal open casket viewings to be comparatively pleasant experiences, but it is not intended for the long-term preservation of the remains. That is why funeral providers are legally prohibited from making any claims about the long-term preservative effects of embalming. Similarly, they cannot legally claim that ordinary caskets or burial vaults will prevent decomposition or protect the body from the effects of water and other substances in the ground.

Funeral directors sometimes charge consumers for what are known as "cash advance" items — for example, charges that are paid to the cemetery but which are collected from the consumer by the funeral director. The Funeral Rule requires that the funeral director make clear in writing both the actual costs for such cash advance items as well as any markup charged or rebate received by the funeral director.

Should you have complaints about your funeral director, you have several options for redress. First, tell the funeral director your concerns and let him or her know you are unhappy. In many cases, that's all it will take to straighten out any problems. If that does not work, most states have statewide associations of funeral directors that act as a self-policing organizations within the industry. Contact them to see if they can help you. States also have state agencies that license funeral directors and, in extreme cases, it may be necessary to complain to the appropriate licensing body. If you feel you have been the victim of fraud or some other criminal activity, you can contact the local district or state's attorney, or the attorney general of the state where you live. Finally, you can also get in touch with the nearest office of the Federal Trade Commission to see if they can help.

At the time of your meeting with the funeral director, you must be given a Statement of Funeral Goods and Services that includes an itemized list of all goods and services you agree to purchase from the funeral director. Even if you have purchased a funeral package for a set price, the statement should include an itemized list of prices for each of the goods and services included in the package. The statement also should specify in writing any legal, cemetery or crematory requirements that may affect the purchases you make. If there is a charge for embalming, the funeral director must include a written statement as to why embalming was necessary, either because the consumer requested it or because of a specific and detailed legal or other requirement. A sample statement will be found in the appendix on page 146.

Before you receive your signed and itemized statement from the funeral director, however, there are a few decisions you will have to make.

Cremation or Interment

The first question to be dealt with is the ultimate disposition of the body. Other cultures have developed some interesting alternatives in regard to this issue. For example, in the mountainous and rocky terrain of Tibet, where earth burial is impractical and wood to build fires for cremation is scarce, it is, or at least once was, the custom for local "morticians" to cut up the bodies of the dead and to scatter the pieces on mountainsides for vultures to eat.

Fortunately, our choice for the disposition of the remains of the dead is a simpler and, for our culture at least, less unpleasant one. There are two basic options: will the body be buried or will it be cremated? Both burial, either in the ground or above ground in tombs or mausoleums, and cremation have long histories and are widespread in practice today. Much of what we know about some of our early ancestors, from the Stone Age Neanderthals to the Egyptian, European and Native American cultures, is the result of uncovering their burial sites. For most Americans, burial is the most familiar form of disposition of the dead, one of which we are frequently reminded by the numerous cemeteries that dot our landscape. Keeping the bodies of the dead relatively intact and burying them in the ground or entombing them in private or public mausoleums is the "normal" practice for most of us, one reinforced by our history. Our American ancestors, great leaders such as Lincoln or simple pioneers, were buried, not cremated, and we still visit the sites where they were interred.

Cremation is a bit more unfamiliar for most of us, something a bit alien, rather unsettling, and only recently have we begun to make room for it in our culture. However, while it apparently is not quite as old as burial, the practice of reducing the body through fire to a pile of coarse ashes is thousands of years old and was practiced by many cultures, including the ancient Greeks and Romans. The practice of cremation began to decline in the western world about 400 A.D. because of the spread of

Christianity. Early Christians considered it a pagan practice. Cremation as we know it today began in the 1870s, with the development of an effective and reliable furnace, known as a retort. Today there are more than one thousand crematories in the U.S. and roughly half a million cremations annually.

In the modern cremation process, the body, generally in a simple but sturdy container to facilitate handling, is placed in a retort where it is exposed to temperatures of 1,800 to 2,400 degrees fahrenheit for two to three hours. The intense heat and evaporation reduces it to three to nine pounds of gritty ashes — primarily bone fragments — depending on the body weight of the deceased. The volume of the ashes of an average person takes up about the same amount of space as a loaf of bread.

Some bone fragments remaining after cremation can be quite large, up to several inches in length, and may remain recognizable as human bone. To reduce the bulk of the remains, and to avoid possible problems should scattered ashes later be thought to be evidence of foul play, some crematoriums routinely pulverize remaining bone fragments. Others do not or do so only if requested. If the ashes are to be scattered, it is important to know whether they contain large bone fragments. Contrary to a common rumor, when a person is cremated his or her survivors receive everything that is left of the remains, not just a "selection" of ashes. Material such as metal, that might be present in dental work, for example, is not returned with the ashes, however. Metal and other materials present along with the body may evaporate or may melt into cracks in the retort. Families may request that dental gold be removed from the deceased before cremation, however there seems little point in such a request. Modern dental gold contains remarkably little gold and is scarcely worth the trouble to try to salvage it.

One item that does need to be removed from a body prior to creation is a heart pacemaker. The battery which powers a pacemaker can explode and cause serious damage and even injury in the high heat of the retort. It is usually the responsibility of the funeral director preparing the body to remove a pacemaker.

In cases of cremation, there is often a legally imposed delay — typically twenty-four to forty-eight hours — between the time of death and the actual time of cremation. This allows authorities at least a minimal amount of time to be sure that the death was not the result of foul play.

Cremated remains are usually returned to the family, often by the funeral director, in a temporary container of cardboard or plastic. They can then be placed in a more permanent container such as an urn, which can cost anywhere from $25 to several thousand dollars.

The cremated remains — which the funeral industry frequently refers to in a rather tacky hybrid, "cremains" — can be disposed of in a variety of ways. One advantage of cremation is that the final disposition can be postponed until long after death, when weather, travel arrangements or other factors will not be a barrier to the participation of everyone who wishes to be present.

In some communities you will find a special facility known as a columbarium designed specifically for cremated remains.

The ashes, in an urn or other container, are placed in a niche in a wall at the columbarium, where survivors can visit to pay their respects to the deceased. Some people choose to bury the ashes at a cemetery, in a mausoleum, or at some other location which may have been significant to the deceased. Still others keep the ashes in a decorative container placed in a convenient location — say, on the fireplace mantel.

Scattering the ashes is another popular option. Most places allow ashes to be scattered anywhere on the land or in water. Because of the intense heat of the cremation process, there is no health hazard associated with cremated remains. Nevertheless, to be on perfectly solid legal ground, it is probably a good idea to check with local authorities — the public health department would be a good place to start — before scattering human ashes.

On the other hand, if the deceased felt especially strongly about his or her ashes being scattered in a locale where the practice is forbidden, and if you feel equally strongly about honoring those wishes, there is probably very little local authorities can do to stop you. Unless you are dealing with a very high security area, or unless your plans call for a very large and ostentatious scattering, it should be fairly easy to accomplish your task without even being noticed, let alone stopped. And once the ashes have been tossed to the wind, there's no getting them back no matter what the rules say.

Ashes are often scattered at a spot that is associated with especially good memories for the deceased, or a more general locale may be chosen — the sea, for example, or a wilderness area. Some cemeteries have areas set aside where ashes can be scattered. In some parts of the country there are services you can hire to take the ashes to particularly remote spots and scatter them for you. More likely, you will want to do the task yourself, perhaps with the assistance and participation of a few close family members or friends. Usually some kind of ceremony, either formal or informal, is performed when the ashes are scattered. Some people prefer to leave some sort of physical reminder at the location where ashes have been scattered. On private property, it may be possible to leave a small plaque behind, for example. Or you might want to plant a tree to serve as a memorial to the deceased.

The choice between cremation and burial may be a cultural or social one. In India, for example, the almost universal practice among Hindus is to cremate the dead on open wooden funeral pyres. In Japan and England, it is estimated that cremation is the preferred method of disposition in about ninety percent of all deaths. In the United States, burial is still the preferred custom, but cremation is making inroads in some areas. In California, for example, the cremation rate is about forty percent, while in other parts of the country it may be ten percent or lower.

Quite often, the choice of cremation versus burial will be an economic one. While it is not always the case, cremation can be the cheapest means of providing for the remains. Where an average adult funeral in 1994 cost upwards of $5,000, cremation can cost from $600 to $1,000, including the removal and disposal of the remains and possibly a minimal service. However, the cost of cremation begins to mount if other traditional funeral elements are added. A full funeral, complete with a visitation with the body in an open casket, can cost more than a direct burial without elaborate services and almost as much as a burial with full services. The only savings a cremation affords over burial when similar services are provided is in cemetery costs and in the partial cost of a casket. When the body is to be cremated, it is not necessary to buy a casket. Caskets can be rented for such purposes, but rental only reduces the cost of the casket by about half. Rental is expensive because the interior of a rented casket must be refurbished before it can be rented again or sold.

The choice between cremation and burial can also be one dictated by circumstances. For example, should the death occur abroad, you may find it impractical and prohibitively expensive to bring the body back to this country for burial, and it may seem pointless to bury it in the country where the death occurred, where family members may never have the opportunity to visit the grave.

In such a case, cremation is both more practical and affordable and allows you to bring the ashes back home for scattering or other disposition.

In most cases, however, choosing between cremation and burial will depend on religious or other personal concerns. Some religions, Orthodox Judaism, for example, do not permit cremation. Roman Catholicism once banned cremation for the faithful but now allows it. Individual preferences may play a role. For example, even in cases where the cost of a traditional funeral and burial is not a burden to the survivors, some people feel that money spent on the accoutrements of such services is a waste.

As with so many issues in dealing with death, the wishes of the deceased should be given the most serious consideration whenever they are known and it is possible and practicable to honor them.

One final factor should be born in mind when cremation is the choice for disposition. Some mourners may be put off or disgusted by some aspects of the process. For example, being invited to participate — or even just to watch others — in the scattering of human ashes may seem gruesome to some people. If you are having services connected with a cremation, be careful to provide an opportunity to take part for everyone who wants to attend, but also give people a graceful opportunity to opt out of any stage of the proceedings that might bother them.

Decisions about the Services

Once you have made your choice between cremation and burial, you will need to make some decisions about what type of services you wish to have. Although a service is not required, there are many reasons for having one. Services give the living a chance to pay their respects to the deceased and to the survivors. They are an opportunity to share grief with other people who cared about the deceased. They are a tangible way to face and accept the reality and finality of death. They offer a ritual framework to mark one of life's most important passages. They provide an opportunity to celebrate the life of the person who has departed.

For these and other reasons, virtually every culture in human history has practiced some sort of death ceremony. In the United States today, a wide variety of ceremonies is available.

The first basic choice is whether the services will be religious or not. This is usually a relatively easy decision, determined by the religious affiliation and beliefs of the deceased and of the survivors. Among religious ceremonies in this country, Protestant services are the most common. Protestant ceremonies vary from denomination to denomination and from church to church. Often, the member of the clergy in charge will tailor the elements of the service to the wishes of the deceased or the survivors — an approach that is also sometimes found in Roman Catholic funerals.

Protestant funerals are generally preceded by a visitation, which can be immediately before the funeral or in the evening a day or more earlier. Most often, the visitation is held at the funeral home, but it can also be held at the residence of the deceased or in another private home. Typically, but not always, the body of the deceased will be present and the casket can be open or closed, depending on the wishes of the family. If it is open, embalming will have been required and some cosmetic preparation of the body will have been done by the funeral director, for a fee. The funeral director may also cut or style the hair of the deceased for viewing, although it is not uncommon for a family to request that a barber or hairstylist who tended to the deceased in life be used. Visitations, with or without an open casket, can be held whether the deceased is to be buried or cremated.

Whether the casket is open or not, the visitation before a Protestant funeral gives friends and family an opportunity to get together, talk informally, express their condolences, and pay their respects. It is common to send flowers to the visitation, although the family may request donations to charity — usually a specific organization or cause — in lieu of flowers. Those attending a visitation will most likely find that a simple expression of regret — such as "I'm so sorry," or "We'll all miss her very much," — are the best things to say. Recounting a favorite memory of the deceased also is often appropriate.

A Protestant funeral will be held at a church and may include prayers, scripture readings, music, the singing of hymns and blessings. In addition to the member of the clergy conducting the service, family members or other survivors may step in front of the congregation to offer a prayer, read a poem or other literary passage or say a few words about the deceased. The acceptability of such a practice will vary from denomination to denomination and from church to church and obviously should be discussed in advance with the minister in charge.

The funeral may be followed by another brief religious service at the gravesite.

Roman Catholic services tend to follow more formal guidelines than some Protestant services but the general pattern is the same. The visitation, often called a wake, takes place on an evening before the funeral, and often includes the praying of the rosary by those in attendance. The recitation is frequently led by a priest. Flowers are commonly sent to the funeral home, or donations to charity are made in lieu of flowers. The casket is usually open at a Roman Catholic wake. The funeral mass is conducted at the church following a fairly rigid pattern. There will be scripture readings and a sermon on the meaning of death and some reference to the deceased. More progressive parishes allow family members or close friends to offer prayers or speak. Communion is given to Catholics who wish to receive it, and hymns and organ music are frequently a part of the service.

Jewish funeral services vary somewhat among Orthodox, Conservative and Reformed branches, but the general pattern is for a brief funeral, lasting perhaps twenty minutes, at a funeral home or private home, not at a synagogue. The funeral itself is the beginning of the ceremonies for the dead, rather than the end. Jewish tradition generally calls for burial within twenty-four hours of death, and the more Orthodox branches of the faith do not permit embalming. After the funeral, traditional Jewish families remain at home, where they are visited by friends and relatives, for seven days. Some families may attend religious services every day for the next year as a part of their mourning. The memorial stone or tablet often is not unveiled for some months after the funeral, which provides an opportunity for another gathering of family and friends. The name of the deceased is read aloud during services every year on the anniversary of the death.

If the deceased was affiliated with a particular religion but did not belong to a church or congregation, you may wish to call one or more churches of the appropriate denomination to find a place to hold the funeral and a member of the clergy to conduct it. If the deceased was not actively religious, you may wish to choose a non-denominational or "humanist" ceremony, which may be held at the funeral home, if the remains are to be present. Alternatively, a non-denominational memorial service — a service without the body — could be held in a private home or other location after burial or cremation. In a non-denominational ceremony, a family member or friend may preside while other mourners gather to talk, share music, group singing, readings of poetry or other literature and exchange memories of the deceased.

Since they don't require the presence of the remains and can be held virtually anywhere at the convenience of all those wishing to attend, non-denominational memorial services probably offer the widest scope for imaginative and unconventional commemoration of the dead. For example, the late rock singer Janis Joplin reportedly left money in her will for her friends to attend a party in her memory at a Sausalito, California bar, an event that was said to have been quite successful. Just about any kind of get-together that's legal, and some that are not have probably been the basis for memorial services. As for the cost of such a service, it can be as little as nothing for a quiet, informal gathering up to as much as you want to spend for a gigantic bash.

As far as more conventional arrangements are concerned, your funeral director typically by prompting will help you to make the choices you will need to make in deciding what kind of services you want to have. Among the issues you will need to address are whether or not to have a visitation or wake; if you have one, whether the casket should be open or closed and whether to encourage friends to send flowers, to donate to a charity instead, or to accept both forms of remembrance. You will also need to decide whether you want the services to be open to all who wish to attend or prefer them to be private.

You will need to discuss any religious service in advance with the priest, minister, rabbi or other member of the clergy. In some cases, the scheduling of the funeral service may depend on other ceremonies already planned at the selected church. You may want to hold the religious service at the funeral home, instead of in church. You will want to ask the member of the clergy in charge what the format will be, and whether family and friends may take an active role. You may also want to request that certain hymns or other music be played at specific times in the service. In some cases, but not always, you may also be allowed to choose the organist or vocal soloist. If the member of clergy did not know the deceased well, you will want to talk with him or her about what kind of a person the departed was, his interests, outlook on life, special characteristics or activities. This will give the officiating member of the clergy information to personalize the eulogy.

If you're planning on giving the eulogy yourself, you'll need to set aside some time to compose your remarks. Think about the things you remember best about the deceased, including special occasions or interests you might have shared and those qualities that set the deceased apart from everyone else you knew. In composing a eulogy, remember the value of brevity. You need not recount every moment you spent with the deceased, or every amusing thing he or she once said. Pick a few representative examples that symbolize the person to you, and keep the speech relatively short.

You also will need to select the pallbearers, who will accompany the casket into and out of the church and to the grave site, or mausoleum. Most of the heavy lifting is usually done by employees of the funeral director, so your choices need not be picked for their physical strength. Close friends and family members are usually chosen as pallbearers. While it is rare for women to be chosen, don't hesitate to ask a woman to be a pallbearer if she was close to the deceased.

If the deceased was a veteran, you may wish to arrange for military honors at the grave site. Many communities have veterans' organizations which provide a color guard and fire a military salute at the cemetery. Veterans' caskets typically are draped with an American flag before burial, with the flag being given to the next of kin just before the casket is lowered into the ground. If you don't know of the appropriate veterans group to contact, your funeral director can help you get in touch with the right parties. If the deceased was a member of a fraternal organization, you may wish to check with that group to see if they provide any special memorial services as well.

Another decision you will need to make is whether or not to have a funeral procession. In its most elaborate form, a funeral procession would begin at the funeral home, proceed in parade formation to the place where the funeral is to be held, regroup after the funeral and go to the cemetery for graveside services. A procession will always include a hearse for the remains, and can include one or more limousines for the family and other mourners. Mourners not riding in limousines use their own automobiles, which are marked to indicate they are part of the procession. Sometimes police, either off-duty or on, are used to provide an escort or to direct traffic. In other cases, no police are used. The extent of the procession you choose will depend on the number and types of services you want, the amount of money you want to spend and the number of mourners you expect.

As you arrange for the services, you will most likely want to see to it that an obituary or death notice is put in the local newspaper. For communities ranging from small towns up to medium sized cities, you will probably find that every death merits a published obituary, which is usually, but not always, printed free. The length and content of a free obituary will vary from newspaper to newspaper. As a general rule, the smaller the newspaper, the longer and more detailed the obituary may be. In larger cities, only celebrities of at least local renown rate obituaries, while ordinary folks must be content with paid death notices, or "morts," as they are sometimes called. Paid death notices have one advantage over free obituaries — you can include as much information about the deceased as you are willing to pay to have printed. That is why people sometimes pay for the printing of death notices even when free obituaries are provided. However, paid death notices usually appear in smaller type than obituaries and are often found in the classified section of the newspaper.

Your funeral director usually will have standard forms for obituaries and death notices that will be accepted by your local newspapers. Among the information that may be included in an obituary is the full name of the deceased, including nicknames where appropriate, age, date and place of birth, date and place of death, parents names, occupation or career, military service, spouse, children, members of the immediate family who died before the deceased and immediate survivors. You may also want to include any special accomplishments of the deceased, either during his or her career, during military service, in connection with volunteer work or in some other field. Educational attainment and membership in clubs, fraternal and service groups or other organizations may also be noted. You may also mention when and where the funeral and other services will be held, what funeral home is in charge of the arrangements, what member of the clergy will conduct the services, the name of the cemetery or notice of cremation and whether flowers or donations to charity are preferred. Other information, such as an expression of thanks to a hospital or a hospice, sometimes is included in obituaries. As a rule, the smaller the newspaper you are dealing with, the more information you can put in an obituary, and the more flexible you can be as to format. In a small town paper, for example, the list of survivors might include the names of grandchildren and great-grandchildren and even nieces, nephews and cousins, while larger papers may have room only to list members of the immediate family.

Perhaps you will wish to send obituaries to, or pay for death notices in, newspapers other than your local one. In cases where the deceased moved to a new locale after living a long time in another community, there may be interest in the person's death in both cities. This is likely to be an increasing concern as more people move from the cities where they have spent their careers to retirement communities that may be thousands of miles away.

Expense

As you make the arrangements for the services, you will be faced with a series of decisions that will determine how much money you are going to have to pay. As you have read earlier, a typical funeral can cost upwards of $5,000, and many people spend far more than that. Even at the $5,000 average amount, consumer advocates argue that the cost of dying is the third largest expense many of us will have in our lifetimes, after buying a home and an automobile. That comparison may not be entirely valid for most of us will own several cars, but funerals are just one to a customer and death does come as a major expense.

Furthermore, it is very easy to make choices that can double the typical $5,000 cost, and if you are very careless, or if money is no object, the sky is the limit as far as price is concerned. For example, while a basic, serviceable, if not very impressive, casket can be had for $400, you will have no trouble finding one that costs $3,000. And although a grave plot, suitable for two graves, can be bought in a small town cemetery for $300, you can also buy a space in a prestigious big city mausoleum for $25,000 to $50,000 — perhaps even more.

Assuming the deceased did not make any funeral and burial arrangements before death, there is a practical limit to the kind of comparison shopping you can do after death. You may be able to check prices at a few funeral homes, but you're not going to be able to shop around indefinitely and get the very best buy. There are, however, some steps you can take to keep costs down.

One of the funeral products with the highest markups, estimated in some cases at twelve times the funeral director's cost, is the casket. To the extent that cost is a factor, do not let yourself be pressured into selecting a casket you cannot afford. Funeral directors may show you only their more expensive caskets. If that happens, look at the casket price list they must furnish you and ask to see less pricey models. Don't be pressured by a sales pitch that suggests that it would be somehow beneath the dignity of the deceased to be buried in a less elegant casket, or that a more expensive model is "more comfortable," or that an expensive casket or vault will keep the body from decomposing. Remember, when someone close to you has died, you are quite vulnerable to attempts to play on any guilt feelings you might have.

You might even want to consider getting a casket from someone other than the funeral director who is in charge of the services. If you are satisfied with him otherwise, but find the prices of his caskets out of line, you might call other funeral homes to find something less expensive. By law, you are not required to buy the casket from the same funeral director who is in charge of the overall arrangements, and he cannot legally tack on a surcharge if you get a casket elsewhere. If you are really into a frugal approach, you could find a carpenter to build a plain wooden box to be used for the burial, or build one yourself if you are at all handy with tools. Remember, too, that a simple concrete slab grave liner, which will probably cost a few hundred dollars, will prevent the grave from sinking in as well as a vault costing several thousand.

You can also cut costs by keeping services to a minimum. If you forego an open casket visitation, you can save on the cost of embalming and other preparation of the body. If you skip the visitation altogether, you avoid the cost of using the funeral directors facilities. And if you opt for an immediate burial, perhaps with a brief service at the graveside, you can trim costs still further.

Cremation with a minimal service is another way to keep costs down. With a direct cremation but with no formal viewing of the body and a memorial service in a home instead, you may be able to get by for $1,000 or less. Remember, though, that adding services adds costs. If you insist on an open casket visitation for a body that is to be cremated, the body will have to be embalmed and you will have to rent a casket.

Even if you do not choose cremation, you should still be able to keep costs down. In 1994, a burial with a full funeral could be had for $3,000 or less in most places.

As you keep your eye on costs, remember that aside from the basics, you don't have to buy any goods or services you don't want. Also remember that there are costs, such as flowers, barbers or hairdressers, honoraria to the member of the clergy conducting a religious service, fees for opening and closing the grave and cemetery lots, that you may have to pay in addition to what you pay the funeral director. Another additional cost is the grave stone or other marker, which can range in price from $300 to several thousand or more. Fortunately, the decision on the marker does not have to be made right away, since the marker most often will not be completed before the burial anyway.

If the deceased did not already own a cemetery plot, this is another decision you will have to make before the funeral. You may be able to make these arrangements through the funeral director, or you may have to visit the cemetery offices. If other members of the deceased's family are already buried in a particular cemetery, you probably will choose the same site for the deceased, if space is available. Or your decision may be dictated by religion because many communities have separate cemeteries for Catholics, Protestants and Jews. In other communities, public cemeteries have separate sections for different denominations. Another factor in choosing a cemetery may be restrictions on the types of grave markers. In some places, only memorial markers flush with the ground are allowed, while other cemeteries permit more traditional headstones. Some cemeteries allow both types of markers in different parts of the grounds. Convenience may be another choice in selecting a cemetery. Ideally, it will be located relatively close to the church, funeral home or other facility where the services will take place, and it also will be at a location convenient for family members to visit in the years to come.

Another option for the burial of a veteran is a national cemetery. If the deceased served in the military, either in peacetime or wartime, in active duty, the reserves or the National Guard, and if they had any kind of discharge other than dishonorable, then the person may be buried in a national cemetery free of any charge. The spouse and any minor children of an eligible veteran may also be buried in a national cemetery. While eligible persons are essentially guaranteed a right to be buried in a national cemetery, they may not always be buried in the one closest to their home and their survivors. Space must be available in a given cemetery, and some, such as Arlington National Cemetery, are closed to all veterans except certain categories of VIPs.

The Veterans Administration will furnish, free of charge, a grave marker for eligible veterans, whether they are buried in a national cemetery or elsewhere. If the burial is not in a national cemetery, however, it will be necessary to request the marker from the VA. The VA may also reimburse a part of the burial expenses of eligible veterans who are not buried in national cemeteries. The VA can also provide veterans' markers for mausoleums and columbaria.

At the same time as you are working to keep costs down, you will also want to be thinking about how you are going to pay for the services you do decide on. For some people, money may not be a concern at all. At the other extreme, where the deceased has left virtually no money or assets and you have your own financial problems, you may wish to check with your state department of public assistance to see if it can provide any monetary aid. Some do.

For most people though, paying for funeral expenses will be a concern, but not an overwhelming one. There may be a burial insurance policy or special life insurance policy that was set aside just to take care of these expenses, for example. In some cases, as when the deceased left assets to cover funeral costs but they are not immediately available because of probate, you may need to work out a payment agreement with the funeral director. Terms can usually be arranged, just as they can be when you make any other large purchase. Sometimes associations of funeral directors will have established their own service to provide credit for paying funeral expenses.

If you do have to work out a payment agreement for funeral costs, check with your state attorney general's office or other appropriate agency to see what restrictions are applied to the funeral director or other source of borrowed funds. Many states, for example, impose limits on the rate of interest that funeral directors can charge.

Checklist

- ☐ Meet with funeral director.

- ☐ Make sure your rights as a consumer are honored.

- ☐ Get itemized price list from funeral director.

- ☐ Decide between cremation, burial or entombment.

- ☐ Decide whether the body is to be embalmed.

- ☐ Decide on the type of services — e.g. visitation, funeral, graveside or memorial services.

- ☐ Decide on cemetery, mausoleum, columbarium or other site for disposition of remains or ashes.

- ☐ Select pallbearers.

- ☐ Prepare obituary or provide information for obituary to funeral director.

- ☐ Make arrangements for payment.

Chapter III
Getting through the services

Once you complete the arrangements for the services, you will find that there are still more details that need to be attended to. Assuming you are the principal survivor — the spouse or other next of kin — most of the decision-making so far has fallen primarily on your shoulders. Most likely there have been friends or other family members on hand to go along with you to the funeral home and to offer support as you make the arrangements for the services. Nevertheless, the responsibility for these important decisions has been yours. Now may be a time to let others carry some of the load. After all, by this point you are still coping with your grief, and you are probably getting a little worn and frazzled from all the work you have been doing. Friends and family will offer to help. Let them. It will make it easier for you and make them feel better for having something tangible to offer you at this time. Delegate where you can some of the remaining tasks that must be done.

Also take time to take care of yourself. You've reached a point now where you can ease off just a bit and devote some energy to making sure you're all right. Don't think of this as self-indulgence or try to prove how strong and stoic you can be. The last thing you want to have happen is that you become sick or exhausted with the funeral and other services still ahead.

Don't be afraid to talk to friends and family about your feelings. Bottling things up won't help you, but sharing them will. It will also help those around you, who are having similar feelings.

Even if you don't feel hungry, eat nutritious foods when you can. As you deal with the many tasks you have before you, your body is burning energy that needs to be replaced. Sweets and other snack foods may be a good source of energy that you can nibble on through the day. Fruits also help provide energy and are healthier. Anything you personally consider a "comfort food" — whether it be meatloaf, hot vegetable soup or a big banana split — will offer both nourishment and emotional sustenance.

Warm drinks like tea and hot coffee will help keep your body temperature normal, but try not to drink too much coffee or other beverages high in caffeine. Also be careful not to drink too much alcohol. A glass of wine, a beer or a mixed drink may help relax you, but stress may make you more susceptible than usual to the effects of alcohol, so take it easy.

Try to rest. Sleep may come easily, and, if it does, don't feel guilty about it. If it doesn't, at least set aside some time for rest in the form of naps or quiet periods just sitting in a comfortable chair. Breathe deeply and try to think about something peaceful and unrelated to the events around you. Even if you don't sleep, your body will benefit from the relaxation and rest. Listening to music, light reading and even watching television may also help you rest and relax.

Things to Do, Things to Do

Among the additional chores that still need to be tended to is the notification of anyone who should be told of the death but has not yet been informed. Your first round of phone calls should have covered the closest friends and nearest family members, but you may have left somebody out. Think again about who might wish to know. Remember that the obituary or death notice, which should appear in the local newspapers quite soon, will take care of casual acquaintances and associates locally. And there will have been a ripple effect as the people you called tell others who in turn tell still others. But what about people who live out of town and won't see the local paper? And what about those distant friends, like old college roommates or service buddies? They may want to know too.

If the deceased was employed and the employer has not yet been notified, now is the time to do so. The deceased may also have participated in volunteer activities where his or her absence will be noticed, or even cause inconvenience. If the deceased maintained a daybook, calendar or other scheduling device, it's probably best to check it to cancel any appointments that are listed, be they business, voluntary or social. Remember, too, that this is the computer age. Many people keep their calendars on a computer or in an electronic organizer or scheduler, so check those too if you need to.

In many cases you can expect that people will be calling to offer their condolences or dropping by to do so in person. It will make things easier for you if you organize family and friends to help answer the phone, greet visitors and take care of food or other gifts people drop off. Be sure whoever handles these chores keeps a list of the names of people who stopped by or called, and any messages or gifts they left. You'll want to be sure to thank everyone who brought any kind of gift later. Thank-yous aren't required for people who simply called or stopped by to offer condolences, but it is a good idea to keep a list of their names as well. After the funeral is over, you and other family members and friends will want to remember those people who took the trouble to be there for you, even in a small way, in your hour of need.

Also enlist volunteers to see to it that your home is tidy. Cleaning the house will be especially important if you plan to have mourners over for an informal reception after the funeral, a common practice. In traditional communities people still bring food to families who have lost a loved one, but there aren't as many traditional communities around as there used to be. Make sure there is food on hand for yourself as well as for visitors. One or two buckets of fried chicken or other quick and convenient fast food can be a lifesaver at times like this. You may want to organize a more elaborate buffet type meal for the reception, or, as an alternative, you could invite close friends and family to a luncheon or dinner at a restaurant after the funeral.

By now you should know who, if anyone, is coming from out of town to attend the services. You will want to make sure that they have accommodations and transportation. Family or friends may offer to house out of town visitors and see to it that they get where they need to go, or the visitors may prefer to stay in a motel or hotel. If they're going to stay in a motel, you may want to have someone local select a comfortable and affordable place and make reservations, rather than letting out of towners take pot luck.

If out of town visitors are going to stay with you or with other family or friends, be sure everything they will reasonably need is on hand. You may have to buy additional sheets, pillowcases and other bedding to make that sleeper sofa in the living room usable. You may also need additional towels to cope with a houseful of people taking showers. Stock up, too, on consumable items such as toilet paper, paper plates, plastic table ware, toothpaste, and bath soap. You also may wish to be sure you have a reasonable supply and selection of coffee, tea, creamer, fruit, breakfast food, juice, soda, and alcoholic beverages and mixers.

Plan well in advance of the services how mourners from out of town will get to the visitation, funeral and graveside services. That means deciding who they will ride with and being sure that both the driver and the passengers know their roles. Out of towners who don't come by car can feel a little stranded if they are dependent for transportation on others. In some cases, depending on your level of trust in the visitors, you may want to offer the use of a car or other vehicle. Often the deceased will have had a car that is available. Depending on your finances, you might also want to think about making a rental car available for the use of out of town visitors.

While you're thinking of transportation, ask yourself if there are any family or friends who will need help in getting to the services or in paying their respects in person before the funeral. Elderly relatives, for example, may have given up driving and have no other convenient way to get to the services. See to it that someone contacts them to make sure they can attend if they wish to.

If the deceased lived alone, or for some other reason his or her home is currently vacant, make sure somebody checks on it. Yes, you had someone attend to any immediate concerns, such as pets that needed tending, shortly after the death. But it's been a few days now, and mail may be spilling out of the mailbox and newspapers piling up on the front porch. Such signs that no one is home are an open invitation to thieves. Make sure someone checks the home regularly. You might even want to have someone "house-sit" until more permanent provisions can be made. If there are items of particular value in an empty home, it might be wise to remove them to the custody of a trusted family member, friend or attorney. If you do that, however, make very sure that a detailed record is kept of who has what. Make equally certain that anyone who may have a legitimate claim to the deceased's estate is aware of the arrangements and agrees to them.

While we're dealing with home security, line up somebody to watch the home of the deceased, and possibly your own residence, during the services. It's not unheard of for professional burglars to use the obituary column to plan their day's work. When the obituary lists the name of the deceased and the time of services, burglars can be pretty sure that the residence will be completely empty for at least an hour or so. All they need is to glance at the telephone directory to get the address. Ask a neighbor who won't be attending the services to keep and eye on things, or find someone who will agree to forego the service to watch the house. If the house being protected is one where mourners will gather after the services, you can accomplish two tasks at once by having someone stay at the house and help get things ready for company.

If the death occurred in a hospital, nursing home or other institution and you haven't already picked up any personal effects there, you will want to have someone do so now. There should not be anything of value, since institutions rightly insist that patients not have valuables for fear of theft. Nevertheless, there may be items of personal or sentimental value that should be collected.

You also will need to arrange for clothing for the deceased to be buried in. While the funeral director can provide clothing, for a fee, it is more common for the family to select a suit, dress or other outfit for the burial. In traditional Jewish funerals, custom dictates that the deceased be buried only in a shroud without pockets.

If the visitation is to be a formal viewing, you may also want to include jewelry. Jewelry can be buried with the deceased, or you can have it returned after the visitation. For sentimental reasons, in the case of the death of a spouse, the survivor may wish a piece of jewelry such as a wedding ring to be buried with the deceased. In other cases, it may mean more to give a ring or other piece of jewelry to a family member or friend, depending on the value of the jewelry and any restrictions imposed by a will. There may also be concern that a valuable item intended to be buried with the deceased may be stolen by funeral workers beforehand. No reputable funeral director would condone such theft, but human venality cannot be denied and the possibility of such thievery cannot necessarily be ruled out.

If an open casket service is planned, you may want to provide the funeral director with a photograph of the deceased. Sometimes, especially in the case of the elderly or of someone who died after a long illness, the person's appearance at the time of death is not the way most mourners will remember him or her. If you wish an open-casket service, one or two good quality photographs of the way the person looked while still fit and healthy may help make the cosmetic work done at the funeral home more effective.

If you anticipate children being at any of the services, particularly quite young children, you may want to designate someone to keep an eye on them. This will not be so important for children who are merely accompanying their parents as they pass through the line at the visitation or attend the funeral. But for children who will be present for longer periods of time, such as children or grandchildren of the deceased who may be at the visitation for the entire period, it will be helpful to have a designated babysitter. Kids can get bored or unruly in such circumstances, and a watchful adult can help keep them from causing problems. Youngsters also will often have a number of questions about the services and about death itself, and it's probably not a bad idea to have someone on hand to answer them as it seems appropriate. Most likely, the person designated to keep an eye on the young kids will be a parent or an older sibling or other relative.

Once all the planning is done and the arrangements are made, getting through the service itself is in some ways relatively easy. Certainly the visitation, funeral and burial are at times profoundly sad moments, moments in which the sense of loss and grief is especially acute. But, in practical terms at least, these are not difficult to navigate and, in most cases, you will have skillful pilots at hand to guide you.

The visitation, typically, is nothing more than a receiving line where you stand or sit to accept the condolences of friends and associates. If the body is present for a formal viewing, it, too, is a part of the line, and the visitors usually stop before it to briefly pay their respects. Conversations are relatively brief, and most people stay just long enough to take their turn in the line. Some close friends and family members may stay longer to offer support. A visitors book is usually provided as a record of those who came to the visitation.

If feelings become too intense or the strain of receiving visitors becomes too much, the funeral home will usually have a private space available where you can sit down and regain your composure. Depending on the number of visitors, the visitation may last two or three hours, or longer.

Whatever the religious denomination of the deceased, or even if there isn't one, the funeral service will follow a fairly predictable pattern, with the clergy, funeral director and others helping you to make your part run smoothly. Often, the family will gather first at the funeral home to view the body one last time, then ride in procession with it to the church or cemetery. The immediate family usually rides directly behind the hearse, which leads the procession. The pallbearers accompany, and usually at least help physically to carry the casket. Typically, they ride together in a separate vehicle. Depending on the decisions you made earlier, some mourners may ride in limousines provided by the funeral director. The remainder will ride in private vehicles.

Jewish funerals are frequently held at the funeral home, or at the home of the deceased, rather than in a synagogue. Christian funerals are usually held at a church according to the rites and rituals of the particular denomination. At the cemetery, a brief ceremony is held at the graveside. Any military honors, such as a ceremonial firing squad and the presentation of a United States flag to the next of kin, are conducted at the cemetery. In some cases, the actual burial may begin with the mourners present as they symbolically toss a handful of earth into the grave. At other times, the burial may take place after the mourners have left.

After all the services have been completed, those riding in vehicles provided by the funeral home are returned to where the day's proceedings began.

As noted in a previous chapter, memorial services which are held after the body has been disposed of, are far more flexible in terms of format than traditional visitations and funeral and burial services. You can do pretty much whatever you feel is appropriate, so there is no way to give even rudimentary guidelines for memorial services here.

In cases of cremation, there may be separate ceremonies, either after the funeral or at a later date, when the ashes are buried, placed in a niche in a columbarium or scattered. Here, too, there can be a broad range of formats, ranging from a fairly traditional burial service for the ashes at a cemetery to a somewhat improvised and free-form scattering ceremony at some special site.

Whatever kind of services you have had, once they are over you may want to direct that any flowers that have been used be taken to nearby hospitals or nursing homes for the enjoyment of the patients there. You can do the same thing with live plants, or they may be given to some of the mourners or taken home. Be sure you collect all the cards that came with any flowers, live plants or floral arrangements so you can send thank-you notes later to the people who sent them.

Depending on the arrangements that have been made and the type of services you have had, immediately after the services may also be a good time to see to honoraria for the clergy, any musical performers involved in the services and anyone else who may have helped, such as the altar boys or girls at a Catholic funeral. In some cases, the funeral director will take care of making some or all of these payments, then add the cost to your bill, but you will want to make sure that anyone who should be paid is paid. If you're unsure of the appropriate amount, you can ask the funeral director or the member of the clergy in charge of the services.

Following the funeral or memorial a reception at the home of the deceased or one of the survivors, or at a restaurant, is a common custom and a way to cushion the impact on the survivors of the completion of the funeral and burial. The reception is one last organized opportunity for the mourners to share their feelings and to celebrate the life of the deceased.

Some time after the end of the reception, it may be necessary to clean the house again, and this is another opportunity for family and friends to offer their help. Out of town visitors may need to be taken to trains or planes, or they may be staying on a few days longer. It is good if they do, because the time immediately after the completion of the funeral ceremonies is often especially difficult. You are emotionally and physically drained and the realization of the real meaning of the loss of a loved one is just beginning to sink in. It is especially important right now to surround yourself with people who care about you.

There are still more tasks to be done before you can honestly say you have taken care of the all the business of dealing with this death. But the sense of urgency has gone. Those things that remain can be done over a period of weeks, even months.

Checklist

☐ Take it easy on yourself — rest, eat properly, etc.

☐ Notify the employer of the deceased and others who should be told.

☐ Arrange for clothing, jewelry, etc. for the deceased. Delegate friends and family to:

    ☐ a) Arrange housing and transportation for out of town guests and others who may need transportation.

    ☐ b) Receive and make notes of food and other items sent to the house.

☐ c) Collect cards and notes attached to flowers sent to funeral home.

☐ d) Tidy the house before and after the funeral.

☐ e) Make sure food, bedding, toiletries and other necessary items are on hand.

☐ f) Keep an eye on young children at the services.

☐ g) Make sure your home and the home of the deceased are secure during the services.

Chapter IV
Taking care of business:
The next several weeks

Once you have taken care of the disposition of the body of the deceased, your next major concern will most likely be the disposition of his or her property. While you will play a role, probably a major role, in seeing to it that this is taken care of, you may have very little say-so in deciding who gets what. If the deceased left a valid will, the directions spelled out in it will determine the disposition of the property. If the deceased died intestate — without a will — the laws of your state will determine the heirs. In either case, you will have no say as to who inherits the property of the deceased. You will be concerned that the matter of inheritance be handled as efficiently and expeditiously as possible, and there are some steps you may be able to take to achieve that aim.

In almost every case, unless the estate is quite small, you will want to consult an attorney. If the deceased left a will, the attorney who drew it up is the most likely one to start with, although you may wish to hire an attorney of your own, as well. The lawyer who drew up the will cannot necessarily be expected to represent your best interest, while a lawyer you hire to represent you is required to. Before meeting with any attorney, however, your first step should be to conduct a thorough inventory of the property of the deceased.

If there is a will, it may list everything the deceased owned or, more likely, it may refer only to certain categories of property, such as real estate, stocks and bonds and cash. The deceased may also have left an inventory of his or her property separate from the will. If not, you should make a list yourself, and, even if the deceased did make an inventory before dying, it may be out of date and in need of revising.

Search the personal papers of the deceased for recent tax returns, check books, savings account pass books, statements from banks or credit unions, and account statements from stock brokers and other financial advisors. Actual securities owned by the deceased, such as stocks or bonds, may have been kept by the owner, in a safe or safe-deposit box, for example, or they may be held by a brokerage firm or other third party. Look for receipts, letters or other records that indicate where securities may be held.

Look, too, for any records that indicate the ownership or partial ownership of real estate or other property, such as cars or boats. Deeds, mortgage records, property tax bills or receipts, licenses and registrations all are indications of ownership of property. Other documents you find may indicate ownership interests in businesses, patents or copyrights that are also a part of the assets of the deceased.

You should understand at this point that anything the deceased owned in joint tenancy with the right of survivorship with someone else, whether that someone is you or a third party, does not become a part of the estate. Rather, the other joint tenant or tenants become full owners of the asset immediately upon the death of the other partner. If a husband and wife, for example, have joint ownership of a bank account or the house they live in, the house automatically becomes the property of the wife when the husband dies, regardless of whether or not he left a will. Joint ownership also means that the jointly owned property is not subject to probate by the courts. Probate is the process in which a local court declares a will to be valid and oversees its administration, including the payment of debts and taxes and the distribution of the remaining property according to the specifications of the will. Typically, the executor named in the will actually handles the details of administering the estate, while the court supervises the executor's actions. When someone dies intestate, probate involves the appointment of an administrator of the estate by a court and the distribution of property according to the laws of the state where the person died.

Probate can be a lengthy and expensive process, so joint tenancy and other legal stratagems are often used to transfer property to a survivor while avoiding the probate court.

Something else you may find in your search of the records of the deceased are insurance policies. Like jointly owned property, the proceeds of a life insurance policy are not a part of the estate. The named beneficiary of the policy will receive the stipulated amount of money according to the terms of the policy regardless of any debts owed by the deceased or any other factors. The other insurance policies — medical, automobile and homeowners, for example — are a matter for the estate's concern. If the deceased died after an illness, for example, there may still be claims to be filed for medical insurance benefits. As another example, you will want to be sure the auto or homeowners insurance policies are continued in effect until they become the responsibility of the new owner of those properties. Call the appropriate insurance agents to be sure that the coverage is continued.

You may also find records of pensions, Individual Retirement Accounts, employee benefit plans and other retirement plans. Add these to your list and ask your lawyer where they fit into the estate. Some, such as some pensions, may not be a part of the estate at all but are treated separately, like life insurance policies. Other plans may pay directly to the estate.

Any potentially valuable items owned by the deceased should also be added to your inventory. This could include art work, jewelry, collections of things like guns, coins or stamps. Cameras, stereo systems and other electronic gear can also be valuable. For purposes of settling the estate, they may eventually have to be appraised. Don't worry about that now — if it needs to be done it will be the responsibility of the executor or administrator of the estate — but do include a reasonably detailed listing of such items in your inventory.

In addition to the assets of the deceased, you also will encounter evidence of his or her debts. Bills, credit card statements, bank notes and other debts should also be added to your list. These will all need to be paid by the estate, usually before any inheritances can be distributed. While you're looking at those credit card bills, be sure to destroy any credit cards that were used by the deceased. If the only name on the account was that of the deceased, notify the credit card company of the death to stop any further use of the account. Where the name of the deceased was the only one on the credit card account, the remaining balance must be paid by the estate unless the account was covered by a special credit insurance policy. The credit card company can tell you if the account was insured. If your name is also on the account, the responsibility for any remaining balance is yours, not the estate's. Notify the credit card company to delete the name of the deceased and direct future bills to you alone.

In some cases, for example when a working spouse has died, it can be difficult for the surviving spouse suddenly to become responsible for the entire balance of a jointly held credit card account. In such cases, it is best to contact the credit card company to arrange an affordable long term payment plan that involves lower monthly payments than the company would normally require. That is preferable to the alternative scenario — letting the bills pile up until the credit card company contacts you and inquires why it hasn't been paid.

There is something else to be aware of when checking the bills of the deceased. There are unscrupulous people out there who see the death of a stranger as a financial opportunity for themselves. There have been cases of such crooks reading the obituaries to find the names of the newly dead, then sending unwanted merchandise in the name of the deceased, claiming that the deceased ordered the merchandise shortly before he or she died. This is an old scam with an international pedigree. The merchandise can be almost anything, but a particular favorite for these vultures has sometimes been expensively bound Bibles. Perhaps they have discovered that people are more reluctant to return a religious item than they are other merchandise. At any rate, be on the lookout for bills for items that seem out of character with the personality or circumstances of the deceased, and don't hesitate to return any unexpected "purchases" that are delivered in the name of someone who has recently died. Even if he did order the item, he won't be needing it now.

Along a somewhat similar line, cancel any memberships the deceased had in things like book and record clubs before unwanted items start piling up. In fact, it's a good idea to cancel any organization memberships in the name of the deceased.

Other records to look for in compiling your inventory include documents relating to social security. The surviving spouse, and in some cases the minor children, of retired or disabled workers may be eligible for some types of Social Security benefits. You may want to check with your local Social Security office or your attorney to see which, if any, benefits apply to you.

Once you have made as complete an inventory as possible of the financial affairs of the deceased, it's time to make an appointment to see your attorney. Take your inventory, as well as most of the documents listed in it. Don't take valuable items, such as stocks or bonds. Take the original, signed copy of the will, if you have it. An original signed copy is the only valid copy of a will — photocopies have no legal standing — so be careful with it.

Remember, too, that this book is a practical, not a legal guide. Its aim is to prepare you for the issues and problems you will have to deal with, but it is beyond its scope to give you definitive answers to major legal and financial questions. After all, there are fifty states in the United States, and each one has a different set of laws for dealing with inheritance, not to mention federal laws and other legal considerations. Where the deceased had property or assets abroad, a totally different set of laws will apply to them. To deal with the complicated legal matters associated with a death, the best advice is to find an attorney you have confidence in and follow that person's advice, never hesitating to ask questions when you don't understand the whys and wherefores of that advice. In a complicated estate with property and assets in several states or abroad, you could even wind up employing the services of more than one attorney.

Depending on the circumstances, you may also find yourself dealing with the executor or the administrator of the estate. Both titles refer to the same function: seeing to it that the assets of the estate are collected and appraised when necessary, that debts and taxes against the estate are paid, that assets are distributed according to the terms of the will or of state law if there is no will. An executor is named by the deceased in the will. If there is no will, an administrator is appointed by the court. Since the executor was chosen by the deceased, it is likely to be someone known to you. An administrator is more likely to be a stranger. In either case you will generally want to be as cooperative as possible to facilitate the speedy disposition of the estate. Depending on the law of the state you live in and the size and complexity of the estate, the estate may be cleared up fairly quickly or it could take a long time. If the estate is so big or complicated that you need to go through probate it could take a year or more. If the estate is small, perhaps because much of the property of the deceased was held in joint ownership with someone else, it may be possible to avoid probate. Again, in complicated legal matters the best advice is to rely on the guidance of an attorney you trust.

In addition to talking to an attorney, there are other legal and financial matters you may also need to attend to. Depending on the extent of investments, property holdings and other financial interests of the deceased, you may need to meet with his or her financial advisor to get a clearer idea of what assets there are. This will be particularly important if you are inheriting those assets. Also contact the appropriate insurance agents to file the necessary claims on life insurance and other policies. If the death was preceded by hospitalization or illness, be sure all bills for health care have been received before settling with the health insurance company. If your own health insurance was provided by the employer of the deceased, if you were the spouse or a minor child, for example, you will need to contact the employer's personnel office to see if, and under what conditions, that coverage can be continued. Or you may need to make arrangements to get your own health insurance coverage. If the deceased died as the result of a work-incurred accident or occupational disease, the surviving spouse and any minor children may be entitled to payment from the state Workers' Compensation office. Check with them if it is appropriate.

Other miscellaneous items that you may need to take care of after the funeral include cancelling magazine subscriptions and arranging for any necessary changes in mail delivery. If you don't live in the same residence as the deceased did, and if you're going to be responsible for handling any remaining business for the estate, you may want to transfer the mail delivery for the deceased to your own home. Alternatively, mail may be need to be routed to the executor or administrator of the estate until it is settled. Once the estate is settled, you can notify the Post Office that the person has died and end all mail delivery. On the other hand, if it was your husband who died, particularly if you are older, you may prefer to continue to receive mail addressed to your husband so as not to draw attention to the fact that you are living alone.

For a number of reasons, including being the principal heir, it may fall to you to dispose of the personal belongings of the deceased, including clothes and other items. You have a number of options here. Charities such as the Salvation Army and Goodwill are often more than glad to receive outer clothing, shoes and similar belongings in good condition. Frequently such charities will even come to your home to pick up such items free of charge. Some people have qualms when they think of a stranger, possibly a down on his luck stranger, wearing the clothing of a dead loved one. They are more comfortable with the idea of passing the items on to a relative or friend who can wear the clothing and get good use out of it. Depending on the condition and style of the clothing, you might also take it to a consignment shop for resale. Clothing that belonged to an elderly person and is noticeably out of fashion might be a welcome gift to a local school or community theater group for use as costumes in period plays. As a last resort, particularly when the clothing is not in very good condition, you can always dump old clothing on the trash pile.

When to decide about the disposition of personal items such as clothing is another question you must answer. Some people must wait a long time after a person has died before they can bear the thought of going through the belongings of the deceased and disposing of them. For example, according to newspaper accounts, after actor Robert DeNiro's father died in the spring of 1993, DeNiro left his father's Manhattan art studio exactly as the elder DeNiro had left it. DeNiro said that at first he did not want to touch anything in the studio. Later, he would just go there and sit. At the time this book was written, more than a year and a half after the elder DeNiro had died, the studio was still just as he had left it.

On the other hand, just as some people feel an extreme reluctance to dispose of the personal effects of the dead, there are others who find it more difficult to face the belongings of a loved one than to get rid of them. For them, it is easier to pile up clothes and other belongings right after the funeral and ship them off to Goodwill. Clearly, the timing of when to dispose of personal belongings is a very personal choice for the survivors.

Personal items other than clothing also can be given to friends and family, donated to charities, sold or pitched, as you choose. One approach that seems to make sense for items that the deceased received as gifts is to offer them to the persons who gave them in the first place.

If the deceased wore eyeglasses, you may want to donate them to a worthy cause, rather than have them lying uselessly around the house. One organization that recycles glasses and frames to indigent people internationally is a group called New Eyes for the Needy. Their address is 549 Milburn Ave., Short Hills, N.J. 07078. Or you might ask your optometrist to recommend another worthy group.

Other tasks that remain to be done after the funeral include arranging for a marker for the grave. This may not always be necessary. If the deceased is joining a spouse who was buried earlier in a joint plot, you may merely need to arrange to add an inscription to an existing marker. In other cases, you will need to visit a monument company to select a marker and provide information for the inscription. Expect to pay several hundred dollars for a very modest marker, and up to several thousand for larger markers made of attractive materials such as marble or granite. Make sure in advance that the type of marker you choose is allowed by the cemetery. Depending on how busy the monument company is, it could take a few weeks to a few months for the marker or headstone to be finished.

If the deceased was cremated and the ashes placed in a columbarium or buried or scattered in a cemetery, you may also want to get a marker appropriate to the site. Traditional grave markers can be used for burial of ashes, while metal plaques are typically used for columbaria or in sections of cemeteries reserved for scattered ashes. If the ashes are to be kept, now may be the time to consider what kind of urn you want. Metal urns shaped like books or cylindrical in form are common, but other shapes and materials are also available.

As you have read earlier, if the deceased was a veteran you may be entitled to receive a marker at no charge from the federal Veterans Administration. These markers are modest in appearance, but include the relevant information about the deceased, including a brief indication of military service. The veterans marker can stand alone or can be in addition to a separate headstone. While you are dealing with the Veterans Administration concerning a marker, you will also want to check on any other veterans benefits you might be entitled to.

If you haven't done so already, you will also want to get a number of certified copies of the death certificate. Most often, you will get these through the funeral director, but if for some reason you can't or choose not to, you can get them directly from the local registrar of deaths, who may be the county clerk, a local public health officer or some other official. The death certificate was filled out at the time the death was reported by the attending physician, coroner or local health officer, and, in most cases, filed with the local death registrar by the funeral director. In most states, you can't even move a body from the place of death to a funeral home, without a death certificate, but your main concern with it doesn't arise until later. You'll need separate copies of the death certificate for a variety of purposes, including applying for life insurance and other death benefits, transferring ownership of property, closing bank accounts and getting access to a safe deposit box. Just as with a will, a photocopy of a death certificate is not acceptable. You must obtain official certified copies from the local death registrar's office, and there will be a fee, probably in the $10 to $20 per copy range. If you get your copies through the funeral director, he or she may or may not add a surcharge to that fee. It's easier to get all the copies you will be wanting at once, so try to make a reasonable estimate of how many you will need. But don't worry if you underestimate. You can always get more later, either in person or through the mail. A sample of a typical death certificate appears in the appendix on page 140.

Still another task after the funeral is to send thank-you cards to people who sent flowers, donated to charities in the name of the deceased, sent food or gifts or did other favors. If you followed the instructions given earlier, you should have lists of the people who brought food and other items along with a stack of cards including the names of people who sent flowers, plants and floral arrangements. If you requested that donations be made to a charity or charities, those organizations usually will promptly send you a list of people who made donations.

Even though there may have been a visitors book at the visitation it is not really required by protocol to send thank-yous to people who attended it, nor are thank-yous expected for people who attended the funeral or graveside service. You may wish, however, to send notes to anyone who was especially helpful — for example, someone who helped to prepare your house for a reception after the funeral or who looked after a vacant house during the services. If you would prefer to have a barber or hair stylist other than one of the funeral home staff prepare the deceased for viewing, a thank-you is in order, as is payment for services and a tip.

Thanks may also go to the clergyman or other person who officiated at the services and to the organist or soloist who performed at the services, particularly if you specifically requested them. If a local veterans group provided a firing squad or other services, you may wish to thank them, as well, and you may want to consider making a small donation to the group.

Thank-yous can be as brief or as lengthy as you want them to be. At a minimum, you'll want to mention specifically what it is the persons did that you are thanking them for — flowers, donations to charity, etc. Anything more you write will depend on your relationship with the person you are writing to.

Thank-you cards may be provided as part of the package you bought from the funeral home, or you can pick up a supply at the local greeting card shop. Thank-you notes can also be written on ordinary stationary, either personalized or not. Handwritten notes are preferred.

Once you've finished the thank-you notes, you may want to gather up the various items connected with the funeral and store them away together in a box somewhere. Items to be stored can include the visitors book from the visitation; the lists of people who called or visited, sent flowers, made charitable donations or sent other items; extra certified copies of the death certificate; a copy of the obituary or death notice; and anything else connected with the funeral you may wish to save.

Checklist

☐ Find the will.

☐ Contact an attorney.

☐ Inventory the property of the deceased.

- ☐ Get a number of certified copies of the death certificate.

- ☐ Check on health, life, auto, homeowners and other insurance policies.

- ☐ Notify credit card issuers.

- ☐ Cancel memberships.

- ☐ Contact financial advisors of the deceased.

- ☐ Contact executor or administrator of estate.

- ☐ Make arrangements for disposition of the deceased's mail.

- ☐ See to it that the debts of the deceased are paid and any remaining assets distributed according to his or her wishes.

- ☐ Arrange for a marker at grave or site where ashes have been disposed of.

- ☐ At the appropriate time, distribute or dispose of the personal effects of the deceased.

- ☐ Acknowledge gifts, food, flowers, personal favors, contributions to charity, etc. with thank-you notes.

- ☐ Store records of death, funeral, services.

Chapter V
Unusual situations

Dealing with death under even the most "normal" circumstances — if such can be said to exist — is stressful and difficult enough. When the circumstances are unusual in any way, the stresses and problems can multiply. Unusual circumstances are most likely to occur when the death is unexpected. When death comes at the end of a period of illness or is the result of old age, it typically is not a total surprise and it usually occurs within the framework of a supportive family, good friends and helpful institutions. When death comes suddenly and unexpectedly, survivors are apt to be less prepared mentally and they may not have ready access to familiar sources of support. What follows is an attempt to consider some unusual circumstances of death and offer some advice for dealing with them.

Death Away From Home

Death away from one's home community is probably more common now than it was some years ago. Certainly, travel is one of the more popular forms of recreation in America and, as the population collectively ages, more and more older people — people closer to their final exit — are away from home more frequently. Freed from the responsibilities of work or of tending to a young family, and often in a financial situation to be able to afford to see a bit more of the world, older Americans as a group are increasing the odds that a sudden event such as a heart attack or an automobile accident may happen to them far from their home towns. Younger people, too, are traveling more than they did a generation or two ago and, while they are less likely to die from a sudden health problem, they are not immune to accidents.

If you are traveling in this country when a husband, wife or other traveling companion dies, you may find yourself feeling totally alone in the world. In a strange community with friends or relatives hundreds or thousands of miles away, dealing with the death of someone close to you may seem to be an overwhelming task.

Fortunately, if you handle things properly, such a situation need not be much more difficult than a death at home would be. Most of the details and decisions that have already been discussed in this book still apply. There are just a few more issues that have to be dealt with.

First, your relationship to the deceased makes a difference. If your traveling companion was a spouse or other close relative, you may be able to act as next of kin and make all the necessary decisions and authorizations. If you are traveling with a friend or distant relative, however, your situation may not be as clear. In many cases, local authorities may allow a relative or friend other than immediate next of kin to claim a body and make funeral arrangements. In other cases they may not. It is also possible that even if the authorities will release the body to you as a distant relative or friend, you may not feel comfortable accepting the responsibility. In such a case, the first thing you need to do is contact the next of kin so that appropriate actions can be taken. For this reason, it's a good idea for everyone to carry the name, address and phone number of their next of kin in their wallet, billfold, purse, or passport, especially when they are traveling.

Assuming you do have the authority to make decisions concerning the remains, either at the site of the death or as next of kin acting from a distance, you will need to deal with the kind of issues that have already been considered in this book, including organ donation, the choice between burial and cremation and the kind of services you wish to have. You also will have to make some decisions dictated by your geographic situation.

Should the remains be transported back home, or should the disposition of the body be taken care of where you are? In most cases you will probably want the body shipped home, but there may be reasons to handle the disposition where the death occurred. For example, if the deceased wanted — or you have decided — to have an immediate cremation with no embalming and no open casket visitation, it's probably just as well, not to mention cheaper and more convenient, to have the body cremated in the community where the death occurred. Going to the expense of transporting the body a great distance, which might very well involve a legal requirement of embalming, makes little sense when it is to be cremated when it arrives at its destination. If you arrange cremation on the spot, so to speak, you may be able to bring the ashes back home with you without any legal problems. Or, if you must return before the ashes are available, you can have them shipped back to your local funeral director where you can pick them up at your convenience. If a memorial service is desired, it can be scheduled later at the convenience of yourself, your family and friends. You can even have the ashes present at the service, if you desire.

Whether you dispose of the remains where the death occurred or plan to bring them back home for disposition there, you will need the services of a funeral director in the community where the death took place. If you have a relationship with a funeral director in your home community, it is probably best to call him or her and ask for a referral to a director where you and the remains are at the time. If it is necessary to transport the body back home, the two funeral directors can work out the details between them. Otherwise, the director you have been referred to can handle all the details there. If you don't have a home-town funeral director you can consult, follow the same procedures for finding one that have already been described. Call a few funeral homes to get an idea of prices and of how open and aboveboard the funeral home staff appear to be. If you are visiting friends and family, you can ask them to recommend the names of reliable local funeral directors. If you are among strangers, you could inquire of the staff at the hotel where you are staying, ask for references from a local church or synagogue of the denomination the deceased belonged to, or ask a local physician who may have attended the deceased or signed the death certificate. The local coroner or medical examiner may also provide a referral, but remember, many coroners are themselves funeral directors and may not be completely unbiased in recommending a funeral home.

Once you have found a funeral director to take charge of the body, dealing with a death away from home usually isn't all that different from doing it on more familiar territory. In making the basic decisions, such as the choice between burial and cremation, the type and number of services and where the services will be held, you can follow the procedures outlined earlier in this book. If the body is to be shipped back home for services, the funeral director in charge of shipping will handle all the necessary steps, so you normally need not worry about providing an escort to accompany the remains. The funeral director also will take care of getting all the necessary permits to ship the body legally. You'll want to make arrangements while you're in the community where the death took place to get a reasonable number of certified copies of the death certificate, since it probably will be easier, quicker and more convenient to get them in person while you are on site than to get them by mail later.

While in most circumstances dealing with a death away from home need not be a great deal more difficult than coping with one on familiar territory, there is one major exception to that rule. When the death takes place outside the boundaries of the United States, making the appropriate arrangements can become extremely complicated. Although 6,000 to 8,000 Americans die abroad each year, death in a foreign country should probably be avoided if at all possible. When not only the laws governing the disposition of the remains, but even your own legal rights, are different from what they are at home, making funeral arrangements can be a major hassle. That is particularly true when dealing with cultures very different from our own, where even the basic assumptions that we make here about the options available may not be valid.

Your position may be especially difficult if you are not permitted to act as the next of kin of the deceased. In that situation, there is very little you can do in concrete terms to take care of the remains or arrange for services. Whether you are next of kin or not, if you are abroad and someone you are travelling with dies, immediately contact the nearest American consulate. If you know the identity of the next of kin, tell the officials there so they can get in touch right away. If you don't know who the next of kin is, the State Department will have to try to find out and make contact. Decisions may have to be made fairly quickly, especially in locales where embalming and refrigeration may not be available. The consulate can also provide help in understanding and meeting local regulations and in securing copies of the death certificate, or its equivalent, and other documentation. Consular officials can also take temporary custody of any property belonging to the deceased and can help make arrangements for the disposition of the remains. However the U.S. government does not provide funds to assist in returning American bodies.

Unless there is some compelling reason to do so, it is probably not a good idea to try to bring a body back from a foreign country. It will be expensive, complicated and possibly traumatic to comply with the various health regulations and other rules. It may even be impossible. To be shipped from overseas, a body must first be embalmed, a procedure not available everywhere. It must them be placed in a hermetically sealed casket packed in a separate outside shipping case. These shipping procedures can cost thousands of dollars, which will be in addition to transport costs and to other funeral arrangements you would make in this country.

Although neither option may be the most desirable under other circumstances, the best choices when someone has died abroad probably will be direct cremation or immediate burial in the country where the death occurred. Of the two, unless there are religious or other objections, cremation may be the best choice. When the body has been cremated, you can have the ashes shipped back home for burial, scattering or other disposition without the legal hassles involved in shipping a body. Depending on your itinerary, you may even be able to bring the ashes back with you. If you do, however, its a good idea to have a certified copy of the death certificate and other necessary documents to present to customs agents when you are asked to explain the ashes.

Be advised, however, that while cremation may be the most convenient form of disposition in dealing with a death abroad, it is not an option everywhere. For example, because their prevailing religion forbids cremation, Islamic countries do not have cremation facilities.

Other situations in foreign countries that you may find troublesome include a shortage of cemetery space in some countries. Unlike the United States, where there appears to be an almost endless supply of potential new cemetery space, some other countries have nowhere to go to find room for new cemeteries. As a result, in some countries — Germany and Greece among them — one who has died and been buried traditionally may be only a short-term tenant in the new grave. After a period of time, that can range from a few years to several decades, bodies are dug up, and the remains placed in a common boneyard or other communal facility. The newly vacated grave is then available for another "tenant."

It should be obvious by now that coping with a death abroad can be an ordeal. If the time comes when you have to face such a situation, about the best you can do is be prepared for the potential difficulties and understand that your options may be extremely limited.

One final bit of advice on this topic. If you find yourself coping with a death abroad, be sure to get plenty of copies of the death certificate or "report of death," as it may be difficult to get extra copies later.

Violent and Sudden Deaths

When someone dies violently, as the result of an accident or crime, for example, or when the cause of death is unknown or suspicious, you will become involved with a set of officials you may have never had contact with before. Most people have had only a limited experience in dealing with the police, of course, what with speeding tickets, fender-benders and the like. But coroners, medical examiners and similar officials are not a part of everyday life for the average individual. They do come into the picture, however, when a death needs to be investigated.

Although they go by several different titles, including coroner, medical examiner and death examiner, officials who investigate violent or suspicious deaths fill essentially the same function. Coroners generally are elected officials, while death examiners and medical examiners are appointed. Coroners and death examiners don't usually need to meet any specific requirements for the job, although they frequently are required to get special training once they have been elected, and sometimes additional training periodically thereafter. Medical examiners usually are physicians, frequently specialists in forensic pathology. It is not uncommon, particularly in smaller communities, for coroners and death examiners to be funeral directors by profession. Whatever their titles, these death officials perform what is essentially a law enforcement function, although the exact nature of their status and authority differs according to the type of official and to the state or local jurisdiction. In some cases, coroners and medical examiners have more authority in dealing with a death investigation than the police themselves, while in other situations their powers are more limited.

A coroner or other comparable official is a background figure who is seldom seen in most deaths. Although doctors, hospitals and nursing homes may be required to inform the coroner of every death that occurs, the coroner does not normally conduct an investigation when someone has died after a long illness or of old age. In the case of a violent death, however, the coroner or one of his deputies typically will be called to the scene at the same time as the police and will launch an investigation that will in part overlap theirs. A medical examiner or coroner may also become involved when a death is sudden or suspicious. If someone with no history of heart disease drops dead of an apparent heart attack, the coroner or medical examiner may decide to investigate. They also may become involved if a child under the age of two dies of unexplained causes.

Once they actively enter a case, coroners and medical examiners typically have considerable authority. They can, for example, take charge of a body and order an autopsy or other tests. An autopsy is a surgical examination of the body to look for signs of disease, injury and other factors. Families frequently oppose autopsies on their loved ones, seeing them as a kind of mutilation of the body. Those fears may be quite justified in at least some cases, but in most jurisdictions a coroner or medical examiner has the authority to order an autopsy or other tests over any objections the survivors might make.

Of course, there may be times when the family very much wants an autopsy to be performed. When the cause of death is suspicious, the family may want every test possible done to find out the truth. If that is the case, they may wish to ask that the local coroner or other death official have an autopsy performed, although the ultimate decision on a government-funded autopsy is usually up to the death official. Families also are free to engage an outside forensic pathologist to perform an autopsy at their own expense. Hospitals also may request that a coroner order an autopsy in cases where hospital officials believe important questions about the death have not been answered. Autopsies may also be required in the case of a death of a child under two where sudden infant death syndrome is suspected as the cause.

Autopsies can be of great value to surviving family members in some cases. Particularly when the deceased has died of an unexpected illness, such as a sudden heart attack when no heart condition was previously known, an autopsy can pick up signs of inherited disease or other hereditary conditions that could affect other family members. Knowing that a potential weakness or condition runs in the family, survivors can be on the lookout for signs of the condition and take precautions to prevent it or moderate its seriousness.

Among the other tests a death official may order are checks for alcohol and other drugs in the blood or tissue of the deceased. These tests can be particularly important in the case of auto accidents and other situations where authorities need to know if drivers and their passengers had been drinking or were otherwise impaired.

As a general rule, death officials can retain possession of a body as long as they need it to complete their examination. Even when they release a body for burial or other disposition, they may retain organs tissue or other body parts for use as evidence in later legal action. If a family wishes to challenge an officials right to retain a body or body part, it may be helpful to hire an attorney to make such a challenge in court. However, even if you hire an attorney, the law will be on the side of the coroner or other death official in most cases.

A coroner or other death official may also delay disposition of a body, particularly by cremation, if there are questions as to the identity of the deceased.

While most coroners and other death officials probably are able, caring and considerate in the performance of their jobs, there are a few who are sometimes guilty of insensitivity in dealing with family members and other survivors. In some cases — for example, where someone is killed because they were driving under the influences of alcohol or because they participated in a crime — it may be painful for family members to admit that a deceased loved one contributed to his or her own death by doing something socially unacceptable. When a coroner or other official is overly brusque or blunt in dealing with such situations, family members frequently take offense. If this happens to you, you may be able to complain to the official's superior and get some satisfaction. In the case of an appointed medical examiner or death examiner, you could complain to the official who made the appointment. With an elected coroner, however, you have less recourse. As an elected official, a coroner is answerable only to the electorate unless his behavior goes beyond the merely offensive and approaches criminal wrongdoing. In that case, the local state's attorney or state attorney general may be the appropriate place to lodge a complaint.

When a medical examiner investigates a death, the investigation itself is generally conducted behind closed doors with the medical examiner issuing his findings as to the cause of death and other details at the end of the investigation. Where a coroner is involved, the process is somewhat more open. After gathering evidence and having the necessary tests performed, the coroner will conduct an "inquest," which is a legal hearing to determine the cause of death. In an inquest, evidence and testimony are presented concerning the circumstances of the death. A coroner's jury hears the evidence and decides on an official cause of death — with the choices typically being restricted to homicide, suicide, natural causes, accidental or unknown causes. A sample form for a verdict of a coroner's inquest will be found in the appendix on page 147.

The finding of the inquest is independent of any criminal action that might be taken concerning the cause of death. For example, a coroner's jury might rule that a death is a homicide, but that does not mean that what we commonly call a murder has taken place. A state's attorney or district attorney might decline to prosecute a case on the grounds of self-defense, for example, or a case might go to trial and the defendant be acquitted. At the same time, a finding by a coroner's jury that death was due to natural causes does not preclude a state's attorney from disagreeing and prosecuting the death — and winning the case — as a homicide.

Generally, family members are notified if an inquest is to be held, and they have the option of attending. While some families may choose to have a member attend an inquest, it is probably more common that they do not.

Checklist

☐ If death occurs away from home, notify next of kin, and follow procedures outlined in previous chapters.

☐ If death occurs in a foreign country, contact nearest U.S. consulate.

☐ Obtain more copies than you expect to need of death certificate or the equivalent because they may be difficult to get later.

☐ Be prepared to deal with coroner or medical examiner, who may order autopsy or other tests in the case of a violent or sudden death.

Chapter VI
Do it yourself?

On the outskirts of a midwestern city a few years ago, workers preparing the ground for a new housing subdivision encountered evidence of previous excavation in the area. They found a series of neatly laid out rectangular holes that had been dug, then filled back in. Because of the shape and pattern of the holes, and because a little was known of the history of the property, it was obvious that this was a cemetery. The graveyard was carefully excavated, and the contents were taken away for analysis. Archaeologists for the state eventually pieced together a fairly complete history of the little burial plot.

It contained twenty-nine graves, and most of the dead were young, under twenty years of age. They had died and been buried in the 1820s, '30s and '40s. The cemetery was a family plot on a family homestead. All the dead apparently died of diseases such as cholera, pneumonia, typhoid and dysentery, which were common on the frontier at the time.

When they died, probably in their own beds, their surviving family members took charge of the burials. They built simple wooden coffins, with no brass plates or handles, no fancy hinges or other adornments, but tapering toward the feet. Many of the dead were wrapped in burial shrouds held together with copper pins. Some of the dead, the younger ones, appeared to have been buried just in shrouds, with no coffins. A few other graves contained buttons and other evidence that indicated some of the dead had been buried wearing regular clothing. Very little in the way of personal effects was found in the graves.

It's easy to imagine this pioneer family lovingly performing the sad final duties for their lost loved ones. Once the person, most often a child, had died, perhaps after a painful illness, they would carefully wash the body, wrap it in a shroud or dress it in a favorite outfit, then gently place it in a newly-made box still smelling of freshly-sawn pine. Perhaps the coffin, its lid still open, would be placed in the front parlour or living room, where loved ones could gather to take one last look at the departed.

Early the next morning, the men in the family would hammer hand-cut nails into the lid of the box, lift it on their shoulders and carry it out to the family plot a short walk from the home. There, they would gently lower it into a grave they had dug by hand, cover it with the fresh earth and say their final prayers. As time passed, family members would no doubt pause occasionally in their daily activities around the farm to visit the graves and to take some solace in the fact that the dead were still a presence in the ongoing life of those left behind.

That's the way it would have been for most of our ancestors — no funeral directors, hired grave diggers, coroners, cemetery managers or others in the business of dealing with the dead. Although there have been professional funeral homes in the United States at least since 1800, most early Americans took care of family funeral arrangements on their own or with the help of friends. What to many today may seem a rather odd and possibly ghoulish ultimate do-it-yourself project was a common fact of everyday life for earlier generations.

There are still groups today — including some Native American, Amish, Quaker and fundamentalist Christian and Jewish communities — who care for their own dead in the time-honored fashion of their ancestors. They and many other people believe that this personal involvement in one of life's most important transitions is both natural and desirable. It helps to define the community and unite it at a time of loss, and reminds its members as well of their links to generations past.

Of course, if you are a member of such a group, you already know this, and if you are not you are unlikely to change religious or ethnic affiliation just for the opportunity to bury your own dead. If you are a member of a close-knit religious congregation or other group with spiritual interests, you might want to consider forming some sort of burial committee to look into the possibility of caring for the group's dead yourselves on a regular basis.

It is also possible for families or individuals who find this more personal approach attractive to become more directly involved in performing the services for the dead. Depending on where you live and the circumstances of the death you have to deal with, you do have the option of taking a more active role in not just arranging the services but carrying them out as well. In some states your role may be limited in certain respects, while in others you may legally be able to do everything those early pioneers did, from preparing and transporting the body to burying it yourself on your own piece of land.

This chapter is not meant to be a comprehensive consideration of all the aspects of the do-it-yourself approach to dealing with death. State and local laws regarding what you can do yourself and how you can or must do it vary widely. If this topic interests you, there are two books that will provide a wealth of information on the topic by two individuals who have first-hand experience in dealing with funerals and burials themselves. The first is "Caring for Your Own Dead," written by Lisa Carlson and published by Upper Access Publishers. Carlson's 1987 book is a thorough discussion of the topic that includes a detailed, if possibly somewhat dated, breakdown of state laws affecting your own ability to take charge of the disposition of a dead person.

The second useful book on this topic is "Dealing Creatively With Death: A Manual of Death Education and Simple Burial," by Ernest Morgan, published by Barclay House. Morgan's book is broader in scope than Carlson's, delving, for example, into questions concerning hospice care for the terminally ill. For that reason, Morgan's book is not as comprehensive in its treatment of the do-it-yourself approach as Carlson's, but it does offer much useful information, including a set of plans and specifications for building your own simple, plywood casket. Both books are available by mail order from the Continental Association of Funeral and Memorial Societies, Inc., 33 University Square, Suite 333, Madison, WI 53715.

If you find the idea of death as a do-it-yourself project an interesting one, there are a number of issues you will have to consider. Check your state or local laws, where applicable, concerning the following topics:

Need for a funeral director. Some state laws require that a licensed funeral director be employed to handle all death arrangements. This would appear to make the do-it-yourself approach impossible, except in some very limited circumstances, such as conducting a memorial service on your own. Other states allow families or religious groups to handle all normal arrangements themselves, while another group of states requires a funeral director to sign the death certificate and to obtain necessary permits, such as for transportation of the body. To the extent that you do use the services of a funeral director, even for a simple matter such as signing a death certificate, you should be prepared to pay a fee.

Death certificate. This is a key document necessary before any disposition can be made of the deceased, and in most cases before a body can even be moved. Depending on the circumstances and the prevailing laws, the attending physician of the deceased, a coroner or medical examiner or other professional may be authorized to sign a death certificate. The death certificate can then be used to get the permits necessary to transport the body and to cremate or bury it. The death certificate must also be registered with the appropriate local death registrar, who may be a town or county clerk or local health officer.

Other permits. Additional permits may be required to transport the body, for burial or cremation. A sample coroner's permit for cremation can be found in the appendix on page 148.

Caring for the body. Even when death is peaceful, a dead body can be an untidy object to have around.

Bodily fluids sometimes leak out after death and should be washed away, for example. If you are caring for your own dead, you should also be prepared to dress the body for burial in whatever way you feel appropriate, be that a simple shroud or the deceased's best dress-up outfit.

Embalming. Embalming is something you cannot legally do yourself, but it may be required for some deaths — for example, when the cause of death was a contagious disease or if you plan to transport the body across state lines. If embalming is required, you will need to hire a funeral director for the job. Expect the fee to include transportation costs and possibly other handling costs as well as the cost of embalming itself.

Holding the body until burial or cremation. If the body is not embalmed, esthetic and sanitary reasons will dictate that you dispose of it promptly, but there is bound to be some time interval between death and disposition. If death occurred at home, in the deceased's bedroom, for example, you may want to leave the body there for a day or so. The front parlor was the traditional place for making a family's dead available for mourners. Modern homes don't necessarily have front parlors anymore, but you may be able to use the living room, a den or other room for the purpose. Bear in mind, too, that there may be local or state regulations that limit how long you can keep a dead body before burial or cremation.

Burial. If the body is to be buried, you must decide how and where. In some places, it is perfectly legal to bury the deceased on private land, a family farm, for example, if local codes are obeyed. Health and other concerns require that certain standards be met, such as that burial be a certain minimum distance

111

from a water supply. If such issues are properly addressed, you will find that it is perfectly legal in some cases to bury Grandmother in the back yard where you can visit her grave daily. Think twice about home burial, though. If there is any chance that the family won't be on the same property for the long term, you may want to opt for a cemetery. If you sell the property and move away, it will be hard to guarantee that future owners don't dig Grandmother up someday to build a new barn. A homemade wooden casket may be acceptable whether burial is on private land or at a cemetery, but if you do choose to use a cemetery, an outer burial container will probably be required to prevent subsidence. A burial permit may be required whether the burial is on private land or in a cemetery.

Cremation. In many places, a separate permit is required for cremation, both as an administrative matter and to prevent the concealment of wrongdoing. There is usually a legally mandated delay period — often 24 to 48 hours — between the time of death and when cremation can take place. In addition, not all crematories will accept bodies directly from families. If you can't find one that will, you may have to hire a funeral director. If you do deal directly with the crematorium, remember that pacemakers must be removed from a body to be cremated. This is a simple process, but if it is overlooked, the result can be a dangerous explosion caused by heating the pacemakers battery. It is up to you to be sure any pacemaker is removed before cremation. If you don't, you could be liable for any damage done by an explosion. The options for disposition of the ashes after cremation are the same as when the arrangements have been handled by a funeral director.

Transportation. Permits may be needed to transport the body.

Ceremonies. This is the one area where the family or other survivors have the most leeway. Even in conventional rituals conducted by a funeral director, the survivors have great latitude as to the type of ceremony, if any, that will be held. There is no need to go to the expense of a visitation or of a funeral with the body present, for example. A private memorial service in a private home after the body has been buried or cremated is an option in any death.

Obituary. If you're handling as many of the arrangements as you can yourself, you'll also want to write the obituary on your own. Look at the section of this book that deals with what information you may want to include in an obituary, then study the newspapers where you will be sending the obituary to determine format and style. Call the papers to find out their deadlines and any other restrictions. Note that in some cases you can fax an obituary to a newspaper, while other papers may require you to bring it in personally, and even provide identification as evidence that the obituary isn't a hoax, before accepting it for publication.

It's obvious at this point that the do-it-yourself approach to caring for the dead is even more complicated than the more traditional method of dealing with a funeral director. It is not something to be entered into lightly, or on the spur of the moment. Considerable research into state and local laws and regulations will be necessary. It will also be a good idea to check with local authorities in advance of the death to let them know you will be handling the arrangements yourself. Most town clerks or other registrars of death certificates are used to dealing with funeral directors, not the family of the deceased. If you show up without warning after the death and ask to register the death certificate, you could cause considerable consternation, which could lead to delays in proceeding with the necessary arrangements.

There are, for that matter, many technical problems that can occur that could complicate your handling of death arrangements yourself. As an example, even though you may be operating completely within your legal rights in taking your recently deceased elderly aunt for burial on a serene piece of property owned by the family, a police officer who stops you because you have a broken tail light might be more than a little suspicious about the dead body in the plywood box in the back of your pickup. What began as a well-intentioned effort to do one final personal service for a loved family member could end up as your first chance to try on a pair of handcuffs and spend a brief but unpleasant stint in the local jail.

Technical preparations aside, you will also want to be sure that you are prepared psychologically for taking charge of things yourself. Most people have never touched a dead body, let alone been faced with the tasks of washing and dressing a deceased loved one, lifting his body into a plywood box, sealing the box and carrying it to a burial place or crematorium. You will want to give the matter some thought before simply assuming that this is a job you can handle without problems.

If all the possible complications and potential problems involved in burying or otherwise disposing of your own dead leave you undaunted, then by all means investigate the matter further. If, however, the idea has absolutely no appeal for you, don't feel bad. It's probably safe to say that there are good reasons why most people prefer to leave most of the major tasks to the professionals.

Checklist

☐ Check local and state laws concerning embalming, cremation, transportation of a dead body, issuance of death certificates, burial and the need for a funeral director.

☐ Make arrangements for the type of personalized ceremony you choose.

☐ Prepare and submit obituary.

Chapter VII
Planning ahead

If you've followed along thus far in this book, it's probably become pretty clear to you that the amount of planning a person does before death has a major effect on how difficult it will be for the survivors to deal with the practical problems of death when they do occur. The more preparation and planning you do to make it clear to your survivors what you want done with your remains, what kind of services, if any, you want and how you wish your estate to be distributed, the easier it will be for them to fulfill those wishes.

Before discussing some of the planning specifics that you ought to be thinking about, it's probably worthwhile to add a caveat about the extent to which your wishes can be enforced after you are dead. Yes, some plans you make concerning what is to be done after your death will have the force of law behind them. While wills can be broken — a fact which accounts for the wealth of many lawyers — a well-made will is not easily overturned. However, other plans you make — for the disposition of your remains, for example — may not be as easily enforced, even assuming there is anyone who is interested in trying to enforce them.

In some respects, once you're dead you no longer have any rights as a person. You become the "property" of your heirs, who are free to make their own decisions as to the disposition of your earthly remains. For example, suppose a man dies leaving instructions that he is to be cremated, with his ashes scattered at his favorite fishing hole. Suppose, too, that the man's wife knew nothing of such plans until the time of death, and she is appalled by the idea of her husband's body being burned. Moreover, she is adamant that the remains be in a specific, identifiable place where she can visit and commune with them — not scattered to the wind and water in some remote locale.

In such a situation, under most circumstances, guess what is most likely to happen to the body! That's right, the wishes of the next of kin prevail. Instead of having his ashes mingled with the fondly-remembered environment of the fishing hole, the husband will probably wind up not cremated but buried, in a metal or wooden box surrounded by a concrete vault in a hole in the ground in a place that had no meaning to him.

More importantly, perhaps, your wishes concerning organ and tissue donations are not binding after your death, either. No matter if you feel strongly that your organs and tissues should be donated for transplantation or medical research, no matter if you have a properly signed and witnessed organ donor card in your wallet. If your survivors feel equally strongly that organ donation is a form of mutilation of the body, then your organs and tissues will be buried or cremated along with the rest of your remains. The consequences in that case can adversely affect many people still living.

The point of this warning is to let you know that it's not enough to make your plans quietly in the solitude of your study, content in the belief that all your wishes will be carried out after your death. It is very important that you let your husband, wife or other next of kin know exactly what you want done and why. This will give you an opportunity to discuss any differences of opinion when minds can still be changed. By the same token, you may want to go beyond your immediate next of kin and be sure that other family members also know how you feel. While it may be enough to guarantee that your wishes are followed if your husband, for example, knows what they are and agrees with them, things may go more smoothly if you take your parents or siblings into your confidence, as well.

For example, Mom and Dad may assume, because of past family custom, that when you die you will be buried in the same cemetery where your ancestors have been buried for generations. You may wish to be cremated. If your spouse agrees to follow your wishes in this matter, then your remains probably will be cremated, all right. But if the idea of cremation comes as a big shock to Mom and Dad, the aftermath of your death may be a major family battle. Better that you had told them beforehand of your plan to break with family tradition.

Keeping in mind the importance of communicating your wishes to your nearest and dearest, it's time to look at some of the specifics you may want to consider as you make plans concerning your own death.

Estate Planning

The first thing most people think about when talk turns to planning for their own death is making out a will and other elements of estate planning. This is logical enough. One of your principal concerns in thinking ahead to your own death is to make sure that the money, property and other things that you have worked hard for in your life are distributed the way you want them to be. A will is generally recommended when your estate is worth more than $600,000, the level where federal estate taxes come into play. But there are other reasons to have a will or to take other legal action to plan the disposition of your estate. One of the most important is to see to it that the various parts of your estate go to the people you wish to receive them.

In the absence of a will or other arrangements, everything you own will be divided up by law according to a formula that varies from state to state.

In most states, if you are married, half to a third of what you own will go to your spouse. Another share would automatically be divided among your children, if you have any. In the event you have no surviving spouse or children, parents, brothers and sisters and other blood relatives generally stand to inherit, in that order. Without a will or other plan, a long-term partner with whom you have a significant emotional relationship can be excluded completely from your estate.

It's easy to envision specific circumstances where dying without a will can be particularly troublesome. Suppose for example, that you're in a close relationship but are not married to the other party. It could be a relationship with someone of the same gender as yourself, in which case a legally recognized marriage is not an option. Or you could be engaged to be married, with the wedding date a year or more off. If you die without a will in such circumstances, your companion loses out to your legal next of kin. That's disturbing enough on the face of it, but it's even worse if your next of kin is someone, a brother or sister perhaps, from whom you are estranged. In that case, not only would your estate *not* go to the person you want it to, it *would* go to the person you might least wish to receive it.

Another situation in which it is vital to have a will is when you have minor children. Without a will naming a guardian for the children, the death of both parents could cause serious problems concerning who takes custody. The worst case scenario in such a situation would be that the children could become wards of your state's child welfare agency — not a desirable prospect in most states.

Although a will is a common way to arrange for the distribution of your property after your death, it's not the only way. Trusts, joint ownership with the right of survivorship and other legal stratagems can also be utilized. In a trust, you can set aside a sum of money or some other asset to be managed by an administrator, known as a trustee. You can arrange, for example, that earnings from the trust be paid to you as long as you live and that, after your death, all the assets of the trust become the property of your designated beneficiary or beneficiaries. Depending on how a trust is established, it may or may not be considered a part of your estate and subject to probate.

Another way to provide for the disposition of property after your death is to make a formal arrangement in which you and someone else jointly own that property. Joint ownership arrangements may be set up in several ways. You can provide that in the event of the death of one owner, all the property immediately belongs to the surviving partner or partners. In such a case, your share of the property does not become a part of your estate. In other cases, jointly owned property is held in what is known as "tenancy in common." In those cases, your share becomes a part of your estate and does not immediately revert to the surviving partner or partners.

Clearly issues such as wills, trusts and joint ownership are complicated ones — complicated enough that many lawyers and other professionals specialize in estate planning alone. For that reason, specific advice about making a will, or planning a trust or jointly owned property are beyond the scope of this book. Hopefully, though, the book will identify some of the questions you need to address, some of the options you have open to you and some of the consequences of dying without making plans for your estate. If you haven't made such plans yet, maybe it's time to see an attorney.

Yes, it is possible to make a will or enter into joint ownership of an asset without involving an attorney. You can, for example, write a perfectly legal will yourself. There are even computer programs that will take you step by step through the process, making allowances for differences in state laws. But legal matters can be complex, and, if you are writing a will or undertaking some other legal action on your own, it would seem advisable at the very least to have a lawyer check the finished product to make sure it will accomplish what you want it to.

Getting Your Records in Order

Whether you have already made a will or made other estate plans or you are just beginning the process, it's a good idea to put together a list of your assets and other important items that will need to be taken care of at the time of your death. As you might expect, this will be a similar procedure to the one discussed in Chapter IV. Whether you're dealing with your own affairs before you die or are taking care of the affairs of someone recently deceased, you can't get those affairs in order unless you have a complete picture of what they are to begin with. So you need the list to make sure every eventuality is covered by your plans. In addition, the list you make will serve as a road map for your heirs and survivors when the time comes for them to take care of your final business.

Your list should include all property you own, either by yourself or jointly with someone else. With jointly owned property, you should also be sure you indicate whether your partners have right of survivorship, meaning they become sole owners of the entire property immediately at your death, or whether the partnership is a "tenancy in common" and your share of the property becomes a part of your estate.

Also include on your list any bank or credit union accounts; stocks, bonds, mutual fund shares and other investments; valuable objects, such as art work or a coin collection you own; any trusts of which you are a beneficiary; any businesses you have an interest in; any cash you have stashed away and any other valuables you can think of. Include, too, any debts that are owed you, pension plans you belong to, retirement accounts you own and insurance policies covering you or your property. Social security, worker's compensation and veterans benefits you are entitled to should also be included, as should any patents or copyrights you own.

In order for your list to be most useful to your survivors after you have died, it should be as specific and detailed as possible. Don't just indicate what stocks and bonds you own, for example. Spell out where the actual certificates are or who is holding them for you. Don't just make note of a valuable coin collection. Leave a record of your best estimate of the value of the individual pieces.

Obviously, a list such as this needs to be updated periodically. Make any necessary changes whenever you acquire a new asset or get rid of an old one. It's also a good idea to check the list regularly, perhaps every year, to be sure there haven't been any changes you have overlooked. A sample list can be found in the appendix on pages 150 – 159.

Keep the list in a secure place. For the sake of privacy and safety, you don't want a complete enumeration of everything you own lying around where anyone can find it. But don't make it so secure that your survivors won't be able to find it when you die. That defeats one of the purposes of making the list in the first place. You might put the list itself in a safe deposit box, then leave a note as to its location in an envelope marked "To be opened in the event of my death" in your top desk drawer. In that same envelope, you will also want to indicate the location of your will. Only the original signed copy of your will is a legal document — photocopies have no legal standing — so you will want to be sure the original is in a safe place.

Something else to enclose in the "To be opened ..." envelope are your instructions concerning the arrangements for your funeral and the disposition of your remains. As we saw earlier, you will be well-advised to have discussed your plans with your next of kin well in advance. But you may also wish to leave detailed instructions in writing in a place where they can easily be found. The last place to put funeral instructions is with your will, because in most cases the will is not opened until well after the body has been buried or disposed of.

Planning Your Own Funeral

A plan for the disposition of your remains and any accompanying services can be as simple or as elaborate as you choose to make, and will depend, in part, on how important certain details are to you. Some people may view their own death as the end of their involvement in the affairs of the survivors. For them, it may be enough to say to their next of kin, "Do whatever is most convenient with my remains. Have the kind of services you will feel most comfortable with."

Other people will insist upon details that will be very important to them. The very basic choice between burial and cremation, for example, is one that most people probably are not neutral about. Some persons will ask that the expense of any services be minimal so as not to be a financial burden to survivors. Veterans may have strong feelings about whether or not they want veterans honors at the burial. Many people take comfort in knowing that a favorite hymn will be sung at the funeral or at the grave. The list of details that may be planned for is endless.

Unless you belong to the "Do what's most convenient for the survivors" school of thought, you will want to leave behind some indication of your wishes. If your ideas are relatively simple — a preference for cremation over burial, for example — it may be enough to discuss them orally with your family. If they are more detailed and specific, it will be best to write them down. Here are some of the things you may want to settle. They have already been discussed in some detail earlier in this book, so we will touch on them in abbreviated form here.*Organ/tissue donation, or donation of entire body to medical research?

- Existence of any pre-paid burial plans, cemetery plots, burial insurance policies, etc.?

- Burial or cremation? If burial, what cemetery? If a cremation, what disposition of ashes?

- What services? Visitation? If so, where, and with or without the body being present? Open casket or not? Type of funeral service, if any? Religious or secular? Where, what church or other facility? Funeral procession? Grave side service? Memorial service later?

- Preference as to pallbearers? A list of more than six people is better, because your first choices may not all be available when the time comes.

- Choice of clergy member or other person to officiate?

- Special elements at the ceremony? Hymns or other musical selections? Military honors? Participation by fraternal or other groups you belong to?

- Information you particularly want included in obituary or death notice? Family? Military service? Special accomplishments? Memberships?

- Preference as to type of casket, grave liner?

- Preference as to flowers at services or donations to charities? Which charities?

- Choice of clothes for burial? Particular items of jewelry to be buried with the remains, or not?

- Concerns about expense? Limit on costs? Particular items to be excluded if too costly?

- Inscription or other information for grave marker?

You may also want to include an alternative plan outlining your wishes in the event you die away from home. If you should suddenly die in a distant state, for example, you may wish to spare your survivors the expense and trouble of bringing your body home for services that would not have posed a problem if you had died closer to home.

Prepaid Plans

In addition to planning the details in advance, you may choose to pay all or part of the expense in advance as well. This can be as simple as having a burial insurance policy, or separate life-insurance policy to help offset costs or as complex as making what's called a "pre-need funeral plan" in which you essentially make and pay for all the funeral arrangements yourself. A pre-need plan can be a way to take much of the burden off your survivors at the time of your death, and the funeral industry promotes pre-need planning on that basis. However, there are also problems associated with this kind of arrangement, so you want to be very careful before entering into one.

In a typical case where you buy a pre-need plan, you sit down with your chosen funeral director and make all the arrangements you would make if you were arranging a funeral for someone else. The only difference is, you're not making arrangements for someone who has just died. You're making arrangements for someone who is alive and presumably quite well — yourself. The same Federal Trade Commission regulations that were discussed earlier apply, including the requirement that you be provided with detailed price lists in advance and an itemized bill when you sign the contract. This is really the best time for comparison shopping among funeral directors, because the urgency of having a body that must be disposed of is not a factor.

In making a pre-need plan, you will enter into a contract with the funeral director that will spell out the funeral services that will be provided, such as embalming, transportation, visitation, and plans for the funeral and burial services. It will also include the type of casket or urn, outer burial container and other funeral merchandise that will be provided at the time of your death. The contract also will specify whether the provision of the funeral services and merchandise is guaranteed or not. A guarantee means that once you have met the terms of the contract, there will be no additional costs for the type of services and merchandise you have chosen, no matter what the prices of such items may be at the time of your death. It should also state that merchandise and services of equal value shall be provided at no additional costs if the specified items are not available at the time of your death.

Cemetery arrangements can also be made in advance, although these usually are not made with the funeral director, but with the cemetery management. Cemetery arrangements typically include the purchase of a plot, with or without provisions for long term maintenance and upkeep, or purchase of a space in a mausoleum or columbarium.

Funding for these plans can be handled in a variety of ways, and can be paid either in a lump sum or in installments. If you pay in installments, a guaranteed funeral may not be available immediately. Payment can be made to an annuity, which allows the money to be invested and the interest earned to offset the increase in prices over time due to inflation. Payment can also be made in the form of premiums on a special life insurance policy, with the proceeds to be paid to the funeral home at the time of your death. A special savings account, in joint owner-ship with right of survivorship between you and the funeral home is another pre-need funding mechanism. Payment to a bank trust is another option. Other types of funding also are available.

While pre-need plans have some advantages, there can also be problems that you should be aware of. If for some reason your family isn't aware that you have a plan, they could wind up making separate arrangements, and all the money you spent would be wasted. Even if your family knows about the plan, they could eventually pay substantial additional money if the plan isn't guaranteed. If you move to a different community, your plan may not be transferrable to a new funeral director in your new home town. Even if you don't move, if you die away from home, there will almost certainly be additional charges not covered by your plan for transportation, embalming and other services. Or, if your survivors elect to have all the arrangements handled in the place where you die, they may get no benefit at all from the pre-need plan you purchased. If you die before making a required percentage of the total payments, the plan may be invalidated. And there is always the risk that the funeral home or other business from which you buy a pre-need plan may not be in business at the time of your death.

It is advisable to check with an attorney when making a pre-need plan with a funeral home or other provider. There are also some questions you can ask on your own to help decide whether such a plan is a good idea for you. For example, you will want to understand very clearly how the plan is to be funded and the relationship between the funding entity — a bank, insurance company or other organization — and the funeral home you are doing business with. In most cases the less the two are connected, the better.

You will also want to ask about any tax considerations. Interest earned on the money in an annuity or trust is taxable. You will want to know, among other things, who pays the tax and whether it will be due annually or at the time of your death. You will definitely want to know if the plan is guaranteed or not, and, if it is, when the guarantee goes into effect. You will also want to know if you can change your mind at any point in time without losing your investment and any earnings, if there is a cancellation fee, and what the penalties are if you miss a payment or are late in making one. Ask, too, about what happens if there is not enough money in your account at the time of your death to pay the full cost of the services as planned. And if there is more than enough money to cover the costs, who gets the excess, and what kind of accounting will be provided to show whether there is money left or not? Be sure to ask about the issue of portability — what happens if you have to relocate? And what happens if you die away from home? Will there be additional charges to bring your body back for burial or cremation? Can any of the money you have paid for your pre-need plan be used to cover funeral costs at the location where you die if that happens away from home? Portability also will be a question to ask the cemetery if you buy a plot in advance. Usually you will be stuck with it unless on your own you can find someone else to take it off your hands. Other questions to ask the cemetery management are whether perpetual care and maintenance is included, and whether other lots are available nearby for other members of your family.

Many states require that anyone selling a pre-need funeral contract be licensed. Find out if your state does and get the license number of the person you are considering dealing with. Almost all states have an agency that regulates the sale of these plans, so even if a license is not required you can usually check with the appropriate agency to see what the state regulations and your rights are. You can also ask if there have been any complaints filed against the funeral director or other business you are dealing with.

After considering all the potential problems, you may decide that a pre-need plan is not worth the effort. You can get some of the same benefits, but not the advantage of locking in a price, by setting up a special savings account in joint ownership with the person who is likely to be making your funeral arrangements. Find out the cost of the kind of funeral you want now, then try to make some kind of estimate for the annual effects of inflation. You can then set aside an amount, to be augmented by interest earned, that should cover at least a major portion of the ultimate costs. You could do the same thing with a life insurance policy or a trust, making the beneficiary the person you expect to make your funeral arrangements. Be sure that person is fully aware of your plans and has a written copy of your wishes. Make certain, too, that this is a person in whom you have complete trust — once you are gone, the contents of the savings account, proceeds of the insurance policy or contents of the trust legally become theirs.

Some other options for planning your own funeral include purchasing in advance some of the merchandise that will be needed. For example, you could pick out and buy your own grave marker, having it engraved exactly as you want it except for the date.

Some people have even chosen their own casket and bought it in advance. In these cases, it is not uncommon for the owner to put the casket into interim service as a piece of furniture. Even a plain wooden box for burial can be stood on end, have temporary shelves installed and be used as a bookcase. And a finely made wooden casket might make quite a conversation piece when used as a coffee table.

It probably takes a person with a very well-developed sense of humor — or with none at all — to be comfortable with putting his or her own coffin on display as a piece of everyday furniture. And there is a certain lack of consideration for the survivors implicit in the idea of depriving them of a piece of furniture they have grown used to. Nevertheless, it's an option you may want to consider.

Funeral and Memorial Societies

A special form of pre-need planning that may appeal to some individuals, but probably not all, involves membership in a funeral or memorial society. Such groups (we will refer to them all as memorial societies for convenience) are locally-based and generally combine a frugal attitude with a minimalist approach to death and its attendant services.

Basically, a memorial society acts as a buying club to find funeral directors who will give bargain rates to members of the society for basic services. For a low — typically $15 to $20 — lifetime membership fee, and sometimes for additional annual dues, members of such societies get access to the low rates as well as to a wealth of information concerning burial and cremation, organ and tissue donation, funeral costs and other matters.

Because of access to the lower group rates, and emphasis on a somewhat austere approach to funeral services, memorial societies say their members can cut the average $5,000 price of a funeral to one-fifth of that. For many people that may be an appealing option. However, there is a cost to achieving such savings that may not seem worthwhile to everyone, particularly those with a more traditional attitude toward death and funerals.

For one thing, most memorial society members opt for cremation for a variety of reasons, including avoidance of the additional expenses involved with burial. Where burial does take place, it is done simply and quickly, with no embalming, no cosmetic treatment of the remains and no open casket visitation. When they are needed for burials, caskets are Spartan, being nothing more than a simple box of wood or other suitable material. Services are usually kept to a minimal, if personalized, level. Many society members prefer to have a memorial service at a church, private home or other location, without the body present. Others choose a simple graveside service or dispense with services altogether.

Another disadvantage to memorial societies is that your choice of funeral directors is limited. In Wisconsin, the home state of the Continental Association of Funeral and Memorial Societies, Inc., there is only one approved funeral home for the entire state. Communities in other states may have more than one approved funeral in the same city.

Memorial societies do offer some portability compared to pre-need plans arranged through a funeral director. With their low membership fees and more than one-hundred-fifty local societies across the country that offer reciprocal services, relocation or death away from home is not usually a problem. However, not all states have memorial societies, so you could wind up being a member of a very distant organization, and dealing with a very distant funeral director, in order to achieve the advantages of belonging to a memorial society.

Memorial societies typically do not ask prepayment for services, nor do they usually allow you to lock in prices now for a death that might occur decades in the future.

Although they are self-governing and autonomous local organizations, most memorial societies do not require active participation from members. If you decide to belong to one, your involvement in its governance and other activities can be as limited or as extensive as you choose.

Checklist

☐ Consult lawyer and/or other officials to plan your estate.

☐ Prepare your will.

☐ Where appropriate, arrange for joint ownership with the right of survivorship for certain of your assets.

☐ Get your records in order and update them at reasonable intervals.

☐ Make any desired advanced arrangements for your death services and their financing. Leave written instructions.

Epilog

My great-great-grandmother, Alice Boland, was born in Ireland in 1814 and died in Lincoln, Illinois, 72 years later. Beyond those simple facts, I know very little of Alice. The only family story of what she was like as a person came from a neighbor of hers, who remembered that when Alice was quite old she could sometimes be seen parading around the front yard of her home wearing the shroud that she would be buried in. Perhaps the neighbors thought it strange, morbid even. But it seems to me to be quite sensible for her to want to know how she would look when her time came. No doubt she wished to look her best at one of the few times in her life when she would have been the center of attention.

I've thought of Alice several times as I worked on this book. As I have been focusing on the practical details of dealing with death, it has occured to me that her actions were practical ones as well, no matter how they seemed to the neighbors. Alice just wanted to be prepared, and being prepared is what this book is all about.

The problems and difficulties that can arise in dealing with the death of someone close to you are almost endless, and there are undoubtedly situations that may occur that have not been addressed in the previous chapters. However, I believe and hope that this book book has covered the vast majority of situations you will face when the time comes to deal with the death of a loved one.

At such a time, the best thing that any of us can have going for us is to have dear friends and loving relatives close at hand to help with both the practical and the emotional burdens we must bear. I wish such comfort to all of you. But wether or not you will face such sad and trying times surrounded by caring relatives and friends, knowledge and preparation can also be invaluable assets.

It has been said that Americans are the only people on the planet who see dying as an option, instead of an inevitability. As a result, we tend not to think about death very often or deeply until we are forced to. I hope this book has shown that there is much to be gained by thinking calmly and rationally about what to do when someone dies. I hope, too, that it has provided you with information that will help you work through the details of death. Perhaps it will prevent you from being taken advantage of, or keep you from making decisions that you will one day regret. And I also hope that it will inspire you to make plans that will make it easier for your survivors when the time comes for you to pass on.

No matter how expected a death is, we are never completely ready when it comes. But if we take the time and trouble to think ahead, we can avoid a lot of the difficulties that can arise when someone dies. It's not morbid to do that kind of planning. It's just common sense.

Alice would have understood.

Bibliography

Patricia Anderson. *Affairs in Order, A Complete Resource Guide to Death and Dying*. Macmillan Publishing Company, 866 Third Avenue, New York, NY, 10022, 1991.

Earl A. Grollman. *Living When a Loved One Has Died*. Second edition, Beacon Press, 25 Beacon Street, Boston, Massachusetts, 02108, 1977.

Rabbi Ron H. Isaacs and Rabbi Kerry M.Olitzky. *A Jewish Mourner's Handbook*. KTAV Publishing House, Inc, Hoboken, NJ 07030, 1991.

Edgar N. Jackson. *For the Living*. Channel Press, an affiliate of The Meredith Publishing Company, 1715 Locust Street, Des Moines Iowa, 1963.

David S.Magee. *Everything Your Heirs Need to Know, Your Family History and Final Wishes*. Dearborn Financial Publishing, Inc., 520 North Dearborn Street, Chicago, IL 60610-4354, 1991.

Judith Martin. *Miss Manners' Guide to Excruciatingly Correct Behavior*. Originally published by Atheneum Publishers, 597 Fifth Avenue, New York NY, 10017 it is now published by arrangement with Warner Books Inc, 666 Fifth Avenue, New York NY, 10103, 1982.

Ernest Morgan, edited by Jennifer Morgan. *Dealing Creatively with Death, A Manual of Death Education and Simple Burial.* Twelfth Revised Edition. Barclay House, 39-19 215 Place, Bayside, New York 11361, 1990.

Sheila Simpson. *The Survivor's Guide, Coping with the Details of Death.* Summerhill Press, 52 Shaftesbury Ave., Toronto ON M4T 1A2, 1990. Distributed in the United States by Firefly Books, 250 Sparks Ave. Willowdale ON M2H 2S4.

Lisa Carlson. *Caring For Your Own Dead.* Upper Access Publishers, One Upper Access Road, P.O. Box 457, Hinesburg Vermont, 05461, 1987.

United States of America Federal Trade Commission, Eileen Harrington, Associate Director. *Complying With the Funeral Rule. A Business Guide Produced by the Federal Trade Commission.* Federal Trade Commission, Washington D.C. 20580, 1994.

Granger E. Westberg. *Good Grief,* Revised edition. Fortress Press, Philadelphia, PA., 1971.

Carol Haas, and the Editors of Consumer Reports Books. *The Consumer Reports Law Book, Your Guide to Resolving Everyday Legal Problems.* Consumers Union of the United States, Inc. Yonkers New York, 10703, 1994.

Appendix

All death certificates are based on the same standard federal format, although there are slight variations from state to state. This is the form for Illinois.

| PERMANENT CERTIFICATE ☐ | REGISTRATION DISTRICT NO | STATE OF ILLINOIS | STATE FILE NUMBER |
| TEMPORARY CERTIFICATE ☒☒ | REGISTERED NUMBER | **MEDICAL EXAMINER'S – CORONER'S CERTIFICATE OF DEATH** | |

Type, or Print in PERMANENT INK
See Coroner's or Funeral Directors Handbook for INSTRUCTIONS

| DECEASED-NAME   FIRST   MIDDLE   LAST | SFX | DATE OF DEATH   (MONTH DAY YEAR) |
| 1 | 2 | 3 |

| COUNTY OF DEATH | AGE-LAST BIRTHDAY (YRS) | UNDER 1 YEAR MOS DAYS | UNDER 1 DAY HOURS MIN | DATE OF BIRTH (MONTH DAY YEAR) |
| 4 | 5a | 5b | 5c | 5d |

A ....

DECEASED

| CITY. TOWN. TWP. OR ROAD DISTRICT NUMBER | HOSPITAL OR OTHER INSTITUTION NAME IF NOT IN EITHER GIVE STREET AND NUMBER) | IF HOSP. OR INST. INDICATE D.O.A OP F MER. RM. INPATIENT (SPECIFY) |
| 6a | 6b | 6c |

| BIRTHPLACE (CITY AND STATE OR FOREIGN COUNTRY) | MARRIED. NEVER MARRIED. WIDOWED. DIVORCED (SPECIFY) | NAME OF SURVIVING SPOUSE (MAIDEN NAME IF WIFE) | WAS DECEASED EVER IN U.S ARMED FORCES? (YES NO) |
| 7 | 8a | 8b | 9 |

B ....
C ....
D ....
E ....

| SOCIAL SECURITY NUMBER | USUAL OCCUPATION | KIND OF BUSINESS OR INDUSTRY | EDUCATION (SPECIFY ONLY HIGHEST GRADE COMPLETED) Elementary-Secondary (0-12)   College (1.4 or 5) |
| 10 | 11a | 11b | 12 |

| RESIDENCE (STREET AND NUMBER) | CITY. TOWN. OR ROAD DISTRICT NO | INSIDE CITY (YES/NO) | COUNTY |
| 13a | 13b | 13c | 13d |

| STATE | ZIP CODE | RACE (WHITE. BLACK. AMERICAN INDIAN. etc)(SPECIFY) | OF HISPANIC ORIGIN? (SPECIFY NO OR YES-IF YES. SPECIFY CUBAN. MEXICAN. PUERTO RICAN etc) |
| 13e | 13f | 14a | 14b. ☒ NO   ☐ YES   SPECIFY: |

PARENTS

| FATHER-NAME   FIRST   MIDDLE   LAST | MOTHER-NAME   FIRST   MIDDLE   LAST |
| 15 | 16 |

| INFORMANT'S NAME (TYPE OR PRINT) | RELATIONSHIP | MAILING ADDRESS (STREET AND NO OR R F D. CITY OR TOWN. STATE ZIP) |
| 17a | 17b | 17c |

1 ....
2 ....
3 ....
4 ....
5 ....

CAUSE

18 PART I Enter the diseases, injuries or complications that caused the death. Do not enter the mode of dying, such as cardiac or respiratory arrest, shock or heart failure. List only one cause on each line.

APPROXIMATE INTERVAL BETWEEN ONSET AND DEATH

Immediate Cause (Final disease or condition resulting in death)	(a)
	DUE TO. OR AS A CONSEQUENCE OF
CONDITIONS, IF ANY WHICH GIVE RISE TO IMMEDIATE CAUSE (a) STATING THE UNDERLYING CAUSE LAST	(b)
	DUE TO. OR AS A CONSEQUENCE OF
	(c)

PART II. Other significant conditions contributing to death but not resulting in the underlying cause given in PART I

| AUTOPSY (YES NO) | WERE AUTOPSY FINDINGS AVAILABLE PRIOR TO COMPLETION OF CAUSE OF DEATH? (YES NO) |
| 19a | 19b |

N ....
P ....
....
H.G. ....
RIF ....
UNK ....

| NATURAL. ACCIDENT. HOMICIDE SUICIDE. UNDETERMINED. (SPECIFY) | DATE OF INJURY (MONTH DAY YEAR) | HOUR | HOW INJURY OCCURRED (ENTER NATURE OF INJURY MENTIONED IN PART I OR PART II ITEM 18) |
| 20a | 20b | 20c   M | 20d |

| INJURY AT WORK (YES/NO) | PLACE OF INJURY (AT HOME. FARM. STREET FACTORY. OFFICE BUILDING. ETC)(SPECIFY) | LOCATION (CITY. VIL. OR TOWN OR TWP. OR RD DIST NO. COUNTY. STATE) | IF FEMALE. WAS THERE A PREGNANCY IN PAST THREE MONTHS? |
| 20e | 20f | 20g | 20h.   YES ☐   NO ☐ |

CERTIFIER

| I CERTIFY THAT IN MY OPINION BASED UPON MY INVESTIGATION AND/OR THE INQUISITION. THIS DEATH OCCURRED ON THE DATE, AT THE PLACE AND DUE TO THE CAUSE(S) STATED. AND THAT | THE DECEDENT WAS PRONOUNCED DEAD ON   MONTH   DAY   YEAR | AT |
| 21a | 21b | 21c |

| CORONER'S - MEDICAL EXAMINER'S SIGNATURE | DATE SIGNED   (MONTH. DAY. YEAR) |
| 22a. ▶ | 22b. |

| CORONER'S PHYSICIAN'S SIGNATURE | DATE SIGNED   (MONTH DAY. YEAR) |
| 23a. ▶ | 23b. |

DISPOSITION

| BURIAL. CREMATION. REMOVAL (SPECIFY) | CEMETERY OR CREMATORY-NAME | LOCATION   CITY OR TOWN   STATE | DATE   (MONTH. DAY. YEAR) |
| 24a. | 24b. | 24c | 24d. |

| FUNERAL HOME   NAME   STREET AND NUMBER OR R F D | CITY OR TOWN   STATE   ZIP |
| 25a. | |

| FUNERAL DIRECTOR'S SIGNATURE | FUNERAL DIRECTOR'S ILLINOIS LICENSE NUMBER |
| 25b. ▶ | 25c |

| LOCAL REGISTRAR'S SIGNATURE | DATE FILED BY LOCAL REGISTRAR (MONTH. DAY. YEAR) |
| 26a. ▶ | 26b. |

VR202 (Rev 1/89)   Illinois Department of Public Health - Office of Vital Records   (BASED ON 1989 U.S STANDARD CERTIFICATE)

GENERAL PRICE LIST

These prices are effective as of [date].

The goods and services shown below are those we can provide to our customers. You may choose only the items you desire. However, any funeral arrangements you select will include a charge for our basic services and overhead. If legal or other requirements mean you must buy any items you did not specifically ask for, we will explain the reason in writing on the statement we provide describing the funeral goods and services you selected.

Basic Services of Funeral Director
and Staff and Overhead .... $_____

> Our services include: conducting the arrangements conference; planning the funeral; consulting with family and clergy; shelter of remains; preparing and filing of necessary notices; obtaining necessary authorizations and permits; coordinating with the cemetery, crematory, or other third parties. In addition, this fee includes a proportionate share of our basic overhead costs.

> This fee for our basic services and overhead will be added to the total cost of the funeral arrangements you select. (This fee is already included in our charges for direct cremations, immediate burials, and forwarding or receiving remains.)

Embalming .... $_____

> Except in certain special cases, embalming is not required by law. Embalming may be necessary, however, if you select certain funeral arrangements, such as a funeral with viewing. If you do not want embalming, you usually have the right to choose an arrangement that does not require you to pay for it, such as direct cremation or immediate burial.

Other Preparation of the Body .... $_____
> [list individual services and prices]

Transfer of Remains to the Funeral Home
(within ___ mile radius) .... $_____
> beyond this radius we charge ___ per mile

Use of Facilities and Staff For Viewing
at the Funeral Home .... $_____

Use of Facilities and Staff For Funeral Ceremony
at the Funeral Home .... $_____

Use of Facilities and Staff For Memorial Service
at the Funeral Home .... $_____

Use of Equipment and Staff For Graveside Service .... $_____

Hearse .... $_____

Limousine .... $_____

Caskets .... $_____ to $_____
> A complete price list will be provided at the funeral home.

Outer Burial Containers .... $_____ to $_____
      A complete price list will be provided at the funeral home.

Forwarding of Remains to Another Funeral Home .... $_____
      Our charge includes: basic services of funeral director and staff; a proportionate share of overhead costs; removal of remains; embalming or other preparation of remains, if relevant; and local transportation.

Receiving Remains from Another Funeral Home .... $_____
      Our charge includes: basic services of funeral director and staff; a proportionate share of overhead costs; care of remains; transportation of remains to funeral home and to cemetery or crematory.

Direct Cremation .... $_____
      Our charge for a direct cremation (without ceremony) includes: basic services of funeral director and staff; a proportionate share of overhead costs; removal of remains; transportation to crematory; necessary authorizations; and cremation if relevant.

      If you want to arrange a direct cremation, you can use an alternative container. Alternative containers encase the body and can be made of materials like fiberboard or composition materials (with or without an outside covering). The containers we provide are a fiberboard container or an unfinished wood box.

    A.   Direct cremation with container
           provided by the purchaser .... $_____

    B.   Direct cremation with
           a fiberboard container .... $_____

    C.   Direct cremation with an unfinished wood box........................... $_____

Immediate Burial .... $_____
      Our charge for an immediate burial (without ceremony) includes: basic services of funeral director and staff; a proportionate share of overhead costs; removal of remains; and local transportation to cemetery.

    A.   Immediate burial with casket provided
           by purchaser .... $_____

    B.   Immediate burial with alternative
           container [if offered]... $_____

    C.   Immediate burial with cloth covered
           wood casket .... $_____

ABC FUNERAL HOME
CASKET PRICE LIST

These prices are effective as of [date].

Alternative Containers:

1. Fiberboard Box .... $_____
2. Plywood Box .... $_____
3. Unfinished Pine Box .... $_____

Caskets:

1. Beige cloth-covered soft-wood
   with beige interior.... .... $_____

2. Oak stained soft-wood
   with pleated blue crepe interior .... $_____

3. Mahogany finished soft-wood
   with maroon crepe interior .... $_____

4. Solid White Pine
   with eggshell crepe interior .... $_____

5. Solid Mahogany
   with tufted rosetan velvet interior .... $_____

6. Hand finished solid Cherry
   with ivory velvet interior .... $_____

7. 18 gauge rose colored Steel
   with pleated maroon crepe interior
   (available in a variety of interiors) .... $_____

8. 20 gauge bronze colored Steel
   with blue crepe interior .... $_____

9. Solid Bronze (16 gauge) with brushed finish
   white ivory velvet interior .... $_____

10. Solid Copper (32 oz.) with Sealer (Oval Glass)
    and medium bronze finish
    with rosetan velvet interior .... $_____

ABC FUNERAL HOME
OUTER BURIAL CONTAINER PRICE LIST

These prices are effective as of [date].

In most areas of the country, state or local law does not require that you buy a container to surround the casket in the grave. However, many cemeteries require that you have such a container so that the grave will not sink in. Either a grave liner or a burial vault will satisfy these requirements.

1. Concrete Grave Liner .... $_____

2. Acme Reinforced Concrete Vault (lined)... $_____

3. Acme Reinforced Concrete Vault
   (stainless steel lined) .... $_____

4. Acme Solid Copper Vault .... $_____

5. Acme Steel Vault (12 gauge) .... $_____

ABC FUNERAL HOME

STATEMENT OF FUNERAL GOODS AND SERVICES SELECTED

Charges are only for those items that you selected or that are required. If we are required by law or by a cemetery or crematory to use any items, we will explain the reasons in writing below.

Deceased:_____

Purchaser:_____

Address:_____

Tel. No._____

_____   _____

Date of Death   Date of Arrangements

Basic Services of Funeral Director and Staff and Overhead .... $_____

Embalming .... $_____

       If you selected a funeral that may require embalming, such as a funeral with viewing, you may have to pay for embalming. You do not have to pay for embalming you did not approve if you selected arrangements such as a direct cremation or immediate burial. If we charged for embalming, we will explain why below.

Other Preparation of the Body

       1. Cosmetic Work for Viewing... $_____
       2. Washing and Disinfecting Unembalmed Remains .... $_____

Transfer of Remains to the Funeral Home .... $_____

Use of Facilities and Staff For Viewing .... $_____

Use of Facilities and Staff For Funeral Ceremony .... $_____

Use of Facilities and Staff For Memorial Service .... $_____

Use of Equipment and Staff For Graveside Service .... $_____

Hearse .... $_____

Limousine .... $_____

Casket .... $_____

Outer Burial Container .... $_____

Forwarding of Remains to Another Funeral Home .... $_____

Receiving Remains from Another Funeral Home .... $_____

Direct Cremation .... $_____

Immediate Burial .... $_____

CASH ADVANCE ITEMS

We charge you for our **services** in obtaining: [specify relevant cash advance items].

Cemetery charges .... $_____

Crematory charges .... $_____

Flowers .... $_____

Obituary notice .... $_____

Death certificate .... $_____

Music .... $_____

Total Cash Advance Items .... $_____

TOTAL COST OF ARRANGEMENTS (including all services, merchandise, and cash advance items) .... $_____

If any legal, cemetery, or crematory requirement has required the purchase of any of the items listed above, we will explain the requirement below:

_____

_____

_____

Reason for Embalming:

_____

Coroner's Inquest

_____, then lying dead, upon the oaths of six good and lawful people of said County, who being duly sworn to inquire on the part of the People of the State of Illinois into all the circumstances attending the death of said _____, and by whom the same was produced, and in what manner and when and where said _____ came to _____ death, do say upon their oaths as aforesaid that the said _____ now lying dead came to _____ death on the _____ day of _____, A.D. _____.

VERDICT STATEMENT

WE, THE JURY, FIND THAT _____ CAME TO _____
                                       name   his/her

DEATH ON _____, AT _____, AT _____,
                   date   time   city or township

WE FIND THAT _____ DEATH WAS DUE TO_____,
                  his/her   medical cause of death

WHICH WAS A RESULT OF_____,
                                     circumstances or incident causing death

WE BELIEVE THE MANNER OF _____ DEATH TO BE _____,
                              his/her   accidental, suicidal, homicidal, undetermined, or natural causes

(OPTIONAL ADDITIONS)

ACCIDENTAL BUT AVOIDABLE: (ON THE PART OF WHOM AND WHY)_____
_____
_____.

IT IS OUR OPINION/RECOMMENDATION THAT: _____
_____
_____
_____.

_____

STATE OF ILLINOIS
COUNTY OF _____

Permit No. _____

Date Issued _____ / _____ / _____

MEDICAL EXAMINER'S / CORONER'S PERMIT TO CREMATE A DEAD BODY

Full Name of Decedent _____

Decedent's Address _____

Date of Death _____ Place of Death _____

Cause of Death _____

Cause of Death Certified by _____

Permission to cremate the body of this decedent at _____

_____
(Name and address of Crematory)

has been requested by _____
(Name and address of funeral home)

Funeral Director's Illinois License No. _____

_____
(Signature of funeral director)

Being sufficiently informed as to the causes and circumstances of the death of the above described decedent, permission is hereby granted to cremate the body as requested.

Date _____ _____ *(Signed)* _____, _____ Medical Examiner / Coroner

(MEDICAL EXAMINER / CORONER – WHITE) (CREMATORIUM – CANARY) (REGISTRAR – PINK) (FUNERAL DIRECTOR – GOLD)

VR-204.1 (8/89r)

148

UNIFORM DONOR CARD

Of_____

Print or type name of donor

In the hope that I may help others, I hereby make this anatomical gift, if medically acceptable, to take effect upon my death. The words and marks below indicate my desires.

I give: (a) ____ any needed organs or parts

       (b) ____ only the following organs or parts

_____

Specify the organ(s) or part(s)

for the purposes of transplantation, therapy, medical research or education:

or

     (c) ____ my body for anatomical study if needed.

Limitations, or
special wishes, if any:_____

Signed by the donor and the following two witnesses in the presence of each other:

_____	_____
Signature of Donor	Date of Birth of Donor
_____	_____
Date Signed	City & State
_____	_____
Witness	Witness

This is a legal document under the Uniform Anatomical Gift Act or similar laws. For further information consult your physician or:

Personal Data of _____

Use a separate form for each individual

PUTTING MY HOUSE IN ORDER

This form is published by the Continental Association of Funeral and Memorial Societies, Inc., 6900 Lost Lake Road, Egg Harbor, WI, 54209, for use by its member memorial societies and the individual members of each of those societies.

The information which follows is to provide survivors with a guide for attending to the legal, tax, funeral, obituary, and other matters after the death of the person named above. Items that do not apply should be omitted. Additional sheets may be necessary and may be added to complete the information provided. This form should be brought up to date at each important change that occurs and reviewed at least once each year. Revisions can be more readily made if pencil is used in filling in the items subject to change.

This is **NOT A WILL** and does not govern the disposition of property after your death. You may wish to consult an attorney and arrange to execute a will in the event you have not already done so.

SECTION I contains information that will be needed immediately at the time of your death. It should be kept where it is readily available to your survivor(s). SECTION II contains information that will be needed later and should be filed with your Will and other valuable papers.

SECTION I   Keep this sheet readily available

The person named below has consented to help make arrangements after my death and to comply with my wishes: *(this is usually a family member, or a close or trusted friend, or perhaps the executor of your estate.)*

Name _____ Phone _____

Address _____

I am a member of the following memorial society and I wish to have my remains cared for through funeral arrangements I have made with them:

Society's Name _____ Phone _____

For prompt assistance after ny death call:

Mortuary _____ Phone _____

Address _____

DATA FOR DEATH CERTIFICATE: The doctor in attendance is officially required to prepare and file a death certificate. The following personal data is usually required:

Name_____
      First   Middle   Last

Address_____

_____
    City   County   State   Zip

Resided in this location since (state year) City_____ ; County_____ ; State_____

Residence is: Inside city limits Yes_____ ; No_____ ; On a farm_____ Yes_____ ; No_____

Sex: Male_____ ; Female_____ Color or race_____ Place of Birth_____

Marital Status: Never Married_____ ; Married_____ ; Divorced_____ ; Separated_____ ; Widowed_____ ; Remarried_____

Date of Birth_____ Social Security No._____ Citizen of what country_____

Father's full name_____ Mother's full name_____

Served in U. S. Armed forces? Yes_____ ; No_____ . State War(s) and dates_____

FUNERAL ARRANGEMENTS: I prefer: Cremation_____ Burial_____ Bequeathal_____

METHOD	TYPE	PLACE	NAME AND LOCATION OF PLACE
Dispose of ashes by:	Urn in niche	Columbarium	_____
	Urn burial	Cemetery	_____
	Urn entombment	Mausoleum	_____
	Scatter	Where permitted	_____
Body to receive	Earth Burial	Cemetery	_____
	Entombment	Mausoleum	_____

If niche, cemetery plot or mausoleum is owned or otherwise provided, list details separately.

(over)

151

TYPE OF SERVICE: Memorial (body not present) _____ ; Conventional (casket open _____ , closed _____)

FOR: Friends and relatives _____ ; Private _____ ; Other _____

AT: Church _____ ; Funeral Home _____ ; Our Home _____ ; Other _____

NAME & ADDRESS OF PLACE TO BE HELD: (If church show denomination)

_____

_____

TO CONDUCT SERVICE: Clergyman, or other _____ Soloist, if any _____

Favorite hymns/music _____

LIMIT EXPENSE TO: Minimum _____ ; Low average _____ ; Average _____ ; Immaterial _____ .

REMEMBRANCES to church or favorite charity. (If you wish to aid the "Memorial Society" movement, you can name your local memorial society, or the Continental Association): _____

MY SAFE DEPOSIT BOX is Number _____ in _____ Bank,

Branch _____ , in _____ , key is located _____

Contents of box belonging to others (explain): _____

Name others that have access to box _____

LAST WILL AND TESTAMENT I have no Will _____ . On (date) _____ I executed a Will.

Location of my will is _____

152

Attach the following data on separate sheet or sheets

OTHER INFORMATION FOR NEWSPAPERS:
Time lived in your community, occupation, employer, organizations of which you are a member, schools attended and degrees or honors received, military service showing honors or decorations, other items of interest as well as names of those that would survive you as of this date. (Don't be bashful, tell about your life, it will be a big help to your survivors.)

FAMILY DATA:
(Some of this information should be included in the obituary) Date and place of marriage to present spouse; domicile on date of marriage to present spouse; children by present marriage (name, sex and birthdate; if married, state married name also). If previously married, indicate termination by death, divorce, annulment; name of former spouse (before marriage to you); children by former marriage (name, sex and birthdates; if children married, state married name, also.).

PEOPLE TO BE NOTIFIED:
List names, addresses and phone numbers.

PROFESSIONALS THAT ASSIST ME:
(Show profession, name, address and phone) Attorney, accountant, backer, investment counselor, life insurance agent, casualty insurance agent, auto insurance agent, doctor, dentist, etc.

BUSINESS OR OCCUPATION:
(If retired, show former occupation) Business or industry; business address, if in business for yourself show your employer Social Security number, if any.

HEIRS:
Next of kin, devisees and legatees (only five principal ones required. Show names, relationships, if related, and complete addresses.)

END OF SECTION I
Additional data is filed with my valuable papers in Section II

This form may be photocopied, or additional copies may be obtained from either your local memorial society or from the Continental Association of Funeral and Memorial Societies, Inc., 6900 Lost Lake Road, Egg Harbor, WI 54909-9231. Enclose $1.00 per set (Sections I & II); 3 sets for $2.00. Please include a business-size, self-addressed, stamped envelope.

Signature _____

Address _____

Date _____
(Change as revised)

Phone _____

153

Personal Data of _____ This form for an individual or couple. Use H for Husband; W for Wife, where applicable

SECTION II   Keep this section with your Will and other valuable papers.

YOUR WILL Everyone should have a will. If you have not made one you are urged to do so promptly, and then bring it up to date as conditions change. It will help avoid much delay, expense and doubt. It also provides for you to distribute your estate in the manner you desire. You will obtain satisfaction and be aiding the cause of the non-profit "Memorial Way" movement if you are able to include in your will a bequest to your local Memorial Society and/or the Continental Association.

SURVIVORS DEATH BENEFITS Many death benefits are unclaimed as the survivors are not informed of their availability. List details as to source and amount where known.

Social Security lump sum benefit _____ . Most covered workers are entitled to benefits under varying conditions. Is your job normally covered under State Workman's Compensation Insurance? _____ . Employers' _____ ; Fraternal organization? _____ . Religious groups? _____ . Trade unions? _____ . Death benefits included in life, health and accident insurance policies? _____ . Other possible sources _____

_____ . Are you currently covered under Medicare? Yes _____ ; No _____ . Veterans of U.S. Armed Forces in certain cases are entitled to death benefits. Are you a veteran of the U.S. Armed Forces? Yes _____ ; No _____ . If yes, state your service serial number _____ , branch of service _____ Dates served _____ , peace time _____ , war time _____ ; Are you now receiving a service pension? Yes _____ ; No _____ ;. If yes, is pension for disability _____ ; length of service _____ ; Other _____

*   *   *

The following items make up a check list of the information your Executor, Lawyer, Accountant and family will need answers to after your death. Some items will not apply to your situation. Where they do apply to you a sheet should be made up with the information and attached to this form on all items to which your answer is Yes, or when you need morespace to explain in detail.

RENTS, PENSIONS, ANNUITIES Do you own any property upon which you receive or are entitled to rent or royalties? Yes ____ ; No ____ . If yes, describe your property rights, lease, contract or royalty source and basis or amount of income derived.

SOCIAL SECURITY BENEFITS Do you now receive S.S. benefits for Old Age? Yes ____ ; No ____ . Survivors? Yes ____ ; No ____ . Disability? Yes ____ ; No ____ . If yes, state monthly amounts $ ____ . Do you contribute toward the preceding annuity? Yes ____ ; No ____ . Is any continuing annuity payable to spouse or other survivors? Yes ____ ; No ____ . Where are policies or contracts located? ____

OUT OF STATE PROPERTY Do you own property in any other state or country? Yes ____ ; No ____ .

GIFTS AND/OR TRANSFERS Have you made any gifts or transfers of the value of $5,000 or more during your lifetime without an adequate and full consideration in money or money's worth? Yes ____ ; No ____ .

TRUSTS Have you created any trusts or any trusts created by others under which you possess any power, beneficial interest, or trusteeship? Yes ____ ; No ____ .

LIFE INSURANCE ON YOUR LIFE Show name of insuring company and address, also name and address of local agent, policy numbers, face amount, beneficiary, who pays the premiums and location of policies. Explain any policy loans you may have.

HEALTH AND ACCIDENT INSURANCE Same general data as for life insurance.

(over)

155

AUTO INSURANCE AND CASUALTY CONTRACT   Same data as for other insurance and also show what property the insurance covers or what other risk covered.

REAL ESTATE   Separate property owned by married persons should be indicated and fully explained giving names, addresses and interest of each joint owner. For each parcel of property show: description of property, deed in name of _____, location of deed, date acquired, how acquired? Purchase ____: Gift ____; Other ____. Cost $ ____. Mortgaged: Yes ____; No ____. Leased: Yes ____; No ____. If real estate contract still owing, show name, address and balance owed to contract holder.

STOCKS, MUTUAL FUND SHARES OWNED   Show number of shares owned, type of shares, name of company or mutual fund, your mutual fund account number, certificate numbers, location of certificate and name of your broker and the brokerage company he represents.

BONDS AND DEBENTURES   Same general data as for stocks and add face amount of the bond, interest rate, and type of bond or debenture.

MORTGAGES AND/OR PROMISSORY NOTES OWNED   Show original amount, date made, name and address of maker, collateral, interest rate, location of documents, assignments or co-signers, etc.

CONTRACTS TO SELL REAL ESTATE OWNED   Full price, down payment, date of contract, name and address of purchaser, interest rate, location of contracts, balance as of what date $ _____, __/__/__.

CASH-CHECKING ACCOUNTS   Show name and branch name, and address of bank, your account number, list names of other signers on account.

CASH ACCOUNTS WITH CREDIT UNIONS, SAVINGS BANKS, & SAVINGS & LOAN ASSOCIATIONS   Show name, branch and address of each depository, your passbook number, type of deposit, rate of interest currently paid, other signers on the account, location where passbooks are kept. Explain any interest of others in any balance.

MISCELLANEOUS PROPERTY OWNED Check only the items you own or in which you own interest and give full details. Interest in a copartnership _____ ; interest in life insurance on life of another _____ ; interest in an unincorporated business _____ ; debts owed to me by others _____ ; amounts due me from claims _____ ; rights _____ ; royalties _____ ; leaseholds _____ ; judgements _____ ; remainder interest _____ ; shares in trust funds _____ ; farm products _____ ; growing crops _____ ; livestock _____ ; farm machinery _____ ; autos _____ ; other _____ ; Real Estate mortgages _____ ; Real Estate contracts _____ ; Notes _____

LIABILITIES Check only the items you owe as of this date: Real Estate mortgages _____ ; Real Estate contracts _____ ; Notes Payable _____ ; Bank Loans _____ ; Credit Union Loans _____ ; Finance Company Loans _____ ; personal loans from friends _____ ; personal loans from relatives _____ ; time payment accounts (where not paid in full each month) _____ . On all of the above liabilities checked indicate where documents are located and attach details.

LAWSUITS Are there now pending any lawsuits against you? Yes _____ ; No _____ . If Yes, explain.

CLAIMS Are there any claims against you which you consider invalid? Yes _____ ; No _____ . Explain in detail.

END OF SECTION II Additional data is filed where readily available, in Section I.

Signature _____

Address _____

Phone _____

Date _____
(Change as revised)

157

Keep this section with your personal papers for use by your survivors.

Location of my will _____

Location of Insurance Policies _____

Executor (personal representative) named _____

My Attorney is _____

I have Bank Accounts at _____ location _____ acct.#

_____ location _____ acct.#

_____ location _____ acct.#

Safety Deposit Box Numbers _____ Banks _____

Location of Safety Deposit Box Key _____

Real Estate Owned _____

_____

_____

_____

_____

Location of Deeds _____

I have the following stocks, bonds, contracts or other valuables at: _____

_____

_____

Other information _____

_____

_____

_____

Signature _____

Address _____

My phone is _____

Date compiled _____
(change as revised)